# ANIMAL PORTRAITS IN WOOD

BY NEAL MOORE

**Fox Chapel Publishing**

1970 Broad Street • East Petersburg, PA 17520

www.FoxChapelPublishing.com

## Dedication

For my daughter, Tracy Lynn Langford, and my son, John Travis Moore. No task is too difficult. You just have to believe you can accomplish it.

## Acknowledgments

A very special thank you to Betty Scarberry, my fiancée, for understanding my frustrations while writing this book and for not being too critical of the sawdust that always seems to migrate upstairs. Also to Shannon Flowers, my favorite critic, and all of the wonderful staff at Fox Chapel Publishing who had a hand in publishing this book. You are super people, and it has truly been a pleasure working with you.

**Alan Giagnocavo**
Publisher

**Peg Couch**
Acquisition Editor

**Gretchen Bacon**
Editor

**Troy Thorne**
Design and Layout

**Greg Heisey**
Cover & Project Photography

ISBN-13: 978–1–56523–293–8
ISBN-10: 1–56523–293–3

Publisher's Cataloging-in-Publication Data

Moore, Neal.
      Animal Portraits in Wood / Neal Moore. – East Petersburg, PA : Fox Chapel Publishing, c2006.

            p. ; cm.

            ISBN-13: 978–1–56523–293–8
            ISBN-10: 1–56523–293–3

            1. Marquetry–Technique. 2. Wildlife wood-carving–Patterns. 3. Woodwork–Technique. 4. Woodwork–Patterns. 5. Animals in art. 6. Portrait sculpture–Technique. I. Title.

TT192 .M66 2006
745.51/2–dc22                                                    0609

To learn more about the other great books from
Fox Chapel Publishing, or to find a retailer near you,
call toll-free 1-800-457-9112 or visit us at *www.FoxChapelPublishing.com*.

**Note to Authors:** We are always looking for talented
authors to write new books in our area of woodworking, design,
and related crafts. Please send a brief letter describing your idea to
Peg Couch, Acquisition Editor, 1970 Broad Street, East Petersburg, PA 17520.

Printed in China
10 9 8 7 6 5 4 3 2 1

# About the Author

Neal Moore began working in wood in 1980, carving decorative decoys, songbirds, and miniature carousel horses. He retired from the U.S. Navy in 1983 as a Chief Warrant Officer 3 after 21 years of service. After working 10 years in the aerospace field in Illinois, he returned to work in his home state of West Virginia, where he retired in 2002. Neal bought a scroll saw in 2003 and soon became fascinated with a woodworking technique called segmented portraiture. His original patterns came to the attention of *Scroll Saw Workshop* magazine, whose editors also recognized his ability to teach others. His *Tiger* was featured on the cover of *Scroll Saw Workshop*'s Fall 2005 issue, and a second article, "Brown Trout Scrollsaic," was published in the Spring 2006 issue. Neal now lives in Cottageville, West Virginia, where he works in his basement shop creating patterns and doing commission work of wildlife and family pets.

# Contents

# A Brief History of Segmented Portraiture

Historically, art produced from decorated wood has been categorized into five basic methods: painting, gilding, engraving, carving, and intarsia. Within these five major categories are subcategories through which artisans express their skills and inspiration. For example, relief carving, chip carving, and carving in the round are all methods, or styles, of woodcarving that produce significantly different decoration to the wood.

The type of art I'm addressing in this book, segmented relief portraiture, is nothing more than a form of intarsia, which is known to have been an art form as early as the eighth century; however, the best early examples are said to be from 15th- and 16th-century Germany and Italy.

The word "intarsia" is derived from the Latin verb *interserere*, meaning "to insert." Traditional intarsia consisted of mosaics created from rare and exotic imported hardwoods. These expensive woods were sliced into tiles and then fitted and set into a bed of glue or mastic to form an inlaid image. The process involved demanding, time-consuming, and painstaking work.

Contemporary intarsia processes have developed on a parallel with art and technology. Since the discovery of perspective drawing with its application to painting and the subsequent evolution of the modern scroll saw, intarsia has rapidly become a popular art form among scrollers. This renewed interest has been sparked in no small part by the published works of Judy Gayle Roberts and the patterns by other talented artisans. Almost anyone who is able to follow a line on a pattern with a scroll saw and has the desire to do so is capable of producing realistic images of people, pets, wildlife, or landscapes from wood.

Segmented portraiture, pioneered by Kerry Shirts, provides additional creative opportunities because the artisan is not limited to a choice of native or exotic hardwoods. Using quality modern wood stains, practically any wood color can be closely approximated, if not duplicated, on soft maple, poplar, or other suitable soft woods. These stains used in conjunction with unstained, light-colored wood can be used to produce chiaroscuro effects, or fantastic contrasts of light and shadow, in portraits and landscapes.

The addition of relief to segmented portraiture brings yet another design element to this art form. Relief refers to raising or lowering certain areas of a pattern to give the finished project a greater illusion of depth. For example, the nose and eyes of a wolf portrait would be elevated more than the ears to make it look like that animal is leaning toward you.

This book, *Animal Portraits in Wood*, provides illustrated instructions and patterns for creating realistic portraits of wildlife in wood that incorporate segmentation and relief techniques. It includes projects that scrollers of all skill levels will find challenging yet fun and exciting to complete.

# USING THIS BOOK

For the first few projects, I've described the entire process from start to finish. These first projects are fairly simple patterns that can be cut by scrollers of varying skill levels. Each step is explained in detail and references the appropriate photograph as a visual aid. All a scroller needs to do to successfully complete these projects is follow the directions in the order provided.

As artists progress through the projects in the book, less detailed instruction is provided for each pattern. The procedure is essentially the same for all of the projects, so only minor differences specific to a particular project are explained in the later pieces. It is recommended that each artist review all of the instructions provided for a project before starting work on a particular pattern. A recommended cutting order and an objective are provided to aid you with each of the first few projects. Staining and relief patterns and a color photograph of the completed piece, especially useful as a staining reference, accompany all of the patterns in the book.

One of the advantages of this form of woodworking is that no two renderings of the same pattern will produce identical results—even from the same artisan. Methods of applying the stain to the segments, the artist's choice of wood, and how the scroller glues the segments in relief provide a lot of artistic freedom and expression, resulting in that one-of-a-kind look to every project. With that in mind, be sure to add your own artistic flair once you feel comfortable with the techniques. So, relax, have fun, and let's get started.

# PART ONE

# BASIC EQUIPMENT

Getting started making segmented relief portraits requires some basic equipment. If you are already familiar with how to operate a scroll saw and have your own workshop, you may have many of the necessary items at hand.

## SCROLL SAWS AND BLADE SELECTION

One of the first pieces of equipment that you'll need to consider, if you don't already have one, is a scroll saw and blades for it. The two questions most frequently asked by beginning scrollers are "What is the best low-priced scroll saw?" and "What is the best blade to use?" There is no one good answer for either of these questions. Volumes of information have been written about scroll saws and scrolling. Comparing the various makes of scroll saws and their features is well beyond the scope of this book, as is a description of the blades offered by their many manufacturers. What I can offer is advice based on my own personal experience and that of other experienced and talented scrollers.

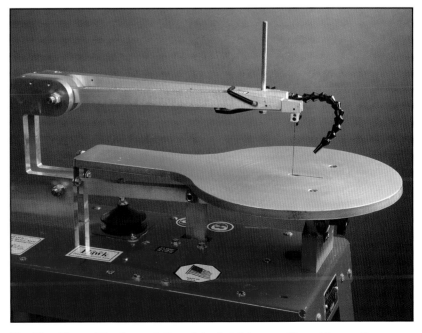

**The First Piece of Equipment.** One of the first things you'll need for creating segmented portraits is a scroll saw.

**Pin vs. Plain.** Choose plain-end blades (bottom) instead of pin-end blades (top).

**Tool-less is Best.** Choose a saw that requires no tools for blade changes.

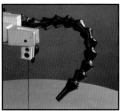

**Get Rid of Dust.** An adjustable dust blower minimizes dust on the pattern lines.

## CHOOSING A SCROLL SAW

I strongly recommend that a beginning scroller purchase the best saw his or her budget allows. If you have the opportunity to try out a saw before buying it, do so. Join a scrolling club, visit a woodworking expo, take a hands-on course . . . Any of these places will give you the chance to try out a saw firsthand.

You want a saw that will accept plain-end, or pinless, blades. Plain-end blades are smaller than pin-end blades and come in a wide variety of sizes and tooth configurations. Their small size allows them to turn and to perform detail work easily. Because plain-end blades don't have a pin to help with alignment, it is especially important to check that a plain-end blade is square to the scroll saw table before you begin cutting.

Pin-end blades, on the other hand, have pins on their ends that fasten the blade to the scroll saw. Because the size of these blades has to be large to accommodate the pin, they come in limited sizes and offer limited tooth configurations. Though pin-end blades can be easier to

align because the pin sits in a slot, they do not perform detail work or turn as well as most plain-end blades.

Additionally, look for scroll saw features such as variable speed, blade changing without tools, adjustable dust blower, and built-in light. An upper arm that lifts up out of the way is essential for top-feeding the blade into fretwork entry holes.

Limited vibration of the operating saw is another very important consideration. Most scrollers will spend several hours in one work session at their saws. Without purchasing the best saw your budget will allow, blowing sawdust, poor lighting, and a struggle to feed the blade through blade entry holes will render the whole scroll sawing experience frustrating. Add vibration into the mix, and you'll get tired quickly.

A good saw is a pleasure to operate. A poor saw creates misery for the user. In my humble opinion, there are no good cheap saws.

## CHOOSING BLADES

Blade selection is a matter of choice—once you gain experience on your saw. There is no one best blade in terms of blade size. Blades are, for the most part, five inches long and numbered from 2 to 12 by their various manufacturers. As a rule, the lower the number, the finer the blade; however, you will find that a #3 blade by one manufacturer may be thicker than a #3 blade produced by another manufacturer.

I used a #5 reverse skip-tooth blade for general cutting and switched to a #2 reverse skip-tooth blade for the more intricate cuts for all of the projects in this book because they are all cut from half-inch poplar.

The size and teeth per inch (TPI) of a blade are chosen based upon the material you are cutting. Thin, soft wood would be cut with a lower-numbered blade, which has many teeth per inch of blade. These blades do not cut as aggressively as the larger-numbered blades

### Features to Consider When Buying a Scroll Saw

- ◆ Accepts plain-end blades
- ◆ Has variable speed
- ◆ Requires no tools for changing blades
- ◆ Has an adjustable dust blower
- ◆ Comes with built-in light
- ◆ Offers an upper arm that lifts out of the way
- ◆ Limits vibration

### Recommended Blade Sizes for Different Types and Thicknesses of Material

| Material | Thickness | Blade Size |
|---|---|---|
| Plywood | ⅛" to ¼" | 2 |
| Hardwood | ⅛" to ¼" | 2 |
| Softwood | ⅛" to ¼" | 2 |
| Plywood | ¾" (stack) | 5 |
| Hardwood | ¼" to ¾" | 5 |
| Softwood | ¼" to ¾" | 5 |
| Hardwood | 1½" and thicker | 9 |
| Softwood | 1½" and thicker | 9 or 12 |

Information courtesy Rick Hutcheson, www.scrollsaws.com

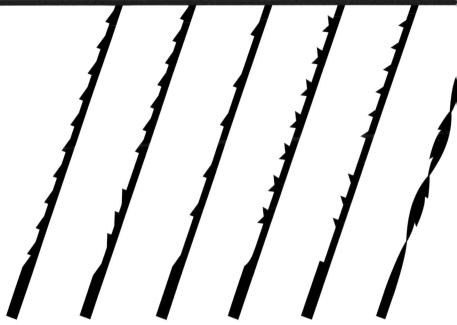

and leave a very narrow kerf, or gap, where the blade has passed through the material. You also have more control when using smaller blades. The larger-numbered blades are generally used for thicker or denser hardwoods. These blades have fewer teeth per inch and cut more aggressively than the smaller-numbered blades.

In addition to size and TPI, blades vary in type within the numbering system. Each kind of blade is designed to perform a different type of work. Following are some general uses for each blade type.

- **Skip-tooth blades** should cut fairly fast and leave a smooth finish.
- **Reverse skip-tooth blades** have several reverse teeth on the bottom of the blade to eliminate tear-out on the underside of the cut.
- **Double-tooth blades** cut fast and leave a smooth finish.
- **Crown-tooth blades** cut on both the upstroke and the downstroke of the blade but generally do not leave a smooth, splinter-free finish.
- **Precision ground tooth blades** claim to leave the smoothest finish.
- **Spiral blades** cut in any direction but leave a rough finish.

There is really no hard-and-fast rule for what specific blade to use. With experience, you will probably find that you can use a #5 blade for work that once required you to use a #3. If you are unfamiliar with blades and the advantages and disadvantages of each, try doing several test runs on a scrap piece of wood.

"Experience" is the operative word here. The more you saw, the better you will become at any type of project you undertake. If you are a beginner, I highly recommend John Nelson's *Scroll Saw Workbook*, available from Fox Chapel Publishing. I also recommend that you visit the *Scroll Saw Woodworking & Crafts* message board at *www.scrollsawer.com*. Hundreds of scrollers of all skill levels participate in this forum, and they will happily answer any questions you may have regarding almost any aspect of scrolling.

Skip-Tooth    Reverse        Double-Tooth    Crown-Tooth    Precision       Spiral
              Skip-Tooth                                     Ground Tooth

## CHOOSING WOOD

Because the final project is stained to show a variety of colors, any light, soft wood will work for the projects in this book. I prefer soft maple. Poplar is also a good choice, and it is commonly available. Good, clear white pine is a third option, but be sure to test it with stain first; it does not always accept stain evenly.

The wood you choose should be at least half an inch thick and sized to fit the pattern you're working on. The wood used in all of the projects in this book is half-inch-thick poplar sized to accommodate the enlarged pattern. Most patterns in this book will fit on readily available boards.

For larger patterns, you may need to cut and edge glue two or more boards together. To do this, begin by dry fitting the boards in the clamps prior to gluing to ensure that the seams will not be visible in the completed portrait. Once the boards are glued, make sure to immediately wipe away any glue that squeezes onto the surface of the wood when you are clamping the boards together. Excess glue that dries on the surface of the wood will seal the wood, making it impossible for the wood to accept stain. Wipe the surface of the wood with a tack cloth to remove any remaining sawdust. Allow the glue to dry for at least eight hours.

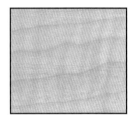

Soft Maple

Poplar

Pine

**Recommended Woods.** Soft maple, poplar, and clear white pine are three light, soft woods that work well for the projects in this book.

**Gather Your Materials.** In addition to a scroll saw, blades, and wood, you'll need a variety of materials. Shown here, clockwise from top left, are cans of wood stain, rubber gloves, paper towels, temporary bond spray adhesive, white acrylic paint, aluminum pans, rags, a drill, drill bits, ¼" luan plywood, black permanent marker, needle-nose pliers, a square, brushes, glue sticks, and a hot glue gun.

## OTHER TOOLS AND MATERIALS

A variety of tools and materials are needed to complete the projects in this book. I recommend that you research and become familiar with these items if you are new to scrolling. Before you begin, gather all of your materials into one area of your workshop. The list provided here includes the general items needed; lists specific to the pieces can be found at the beginning of each project.

**Square:** A square is used to make sure that the scroll saw table and the blade are running at a perfect 90-degree angle. Place the square on the table and move it against the blade. The blade should run alongside the square without pushing against or pulling away from the edge of the square. Adjust your saw to make sure you are running "in square" before you begin cutting; otherwise, the cuts in your project may be off and the final result will be skewed.

**Adhesive:** Temporary bond spray adhesive is an excellent choice for affixing patterns to wood. The bond is strong enough to hold the pattern in place as you saw but weak enough to allow you to remove the paper without too much of a struggle.

**Drill:** A drill press or hand drill is essential for drilling blade entry holes.

**Drill bits:** Choose drill bits that will drill holes just large enough for #2 and #5 scroll saw blades. I use ¹⁄₁₆" bits. The blades will be threaded through these holes to cut interior pattern pieces. If the hole is much larger than the blade, it will be obvious on the finished project.

**Sandpaper:** A little bit of sandpaper is always handy. You may want to sand any fuzz off the pieces once you've finished cutting the project.

**Plywood:** Two pieces of ¼" x 24" x 24" luan come in handy for flipping projects that have lots of very small pieces. Simply lay the project pieces out upside down on one board, place another piece of plywood on top, and use the two pieces to flip the project right-side up.

**Hot glue gun, glue sticks, and wood glue:** I prefer a hot glue gun to hold the segmented pieces together. It dries quickly, allowing the elevated or relieved pieces to stay in place without additional time spent holding the pieces by hand. Make sure you have plenty of glue sticks on hand; you'll use more than you think you will. I also keep wood glue on hand for areas that need extra strength. **Caution:** The tip of the gun and the melted glue are extremely hot and can cause severe burns. Exercise the same caution when using the gun as you would with any hot device and material. Also, hot glue is difficult, if not impossible, to remove from clothing.

**Stain:** Choose a good wood stain to color your projects. I use Minwax Wood Finish, but any good liquid stain will work well. The three colors used for all of the projects are golden oak, dark walnut, and colonial maple. I choose a larger can of stain so I can dip most pieces directly into the wide mouth of the can. The remaining stain can be kept for future projects.

**Marker:** For areas that need to be darker than the stain will allow, use a black permanent marker to color the wood first, and then stain.

**White acrylic paint or gesso:** Use white acrylic paint or gesso to paint the dot that makes the highlight in the eye.

**Gloves:** Rubber gloves will keep your hands clean if you need to stain individual pieces of wood. They also come in handy for moving stained pieces that are not quite dry.

**Needle-nose pliers:** A small pair of 90-degree needle-nose pliers or an old set of ice tongs works well for dipping pieces in stain. They keep the stain off your hands so it isn't accidentally transferred to the unstained segments.

**Brushes:** You'll need a nice selection of small brushes for a technique called smear staining. These can be foam brushes or paintbrushes. If you plan to keep your brushes from project to project, be sure to clean them well after each use according to the manufacturer's directions.

## Tools and Materials

The following is a general list of tools and materials required to complete the projects:

◆ Scroll saw

◆ #2 and #5 reverse skip-tooth blades, plus others of your choosing

◆ Small square

◆ Temporary bond spray adhesive

◆ Drill press or hand drill

◆ Drill bits sized for #2 and #5 blades

◆ Sandpaper, 120 grit

◆ 2 pieces ¼" x 24" x 24" luan plywood, or stiff cardboard

◆ Hot glue gun and glue sticks

◆ Wood glue

◆ Wood stain

◆ Black permanent marker

◆ White acrylic paint or gesso

◆ Rubber gloves

◆ Small pair of 90-degree needle-nose pliers or an old set of ice tongs

◆ Small foam brushes or paintbrushes

◆ Large, disposable aluminum baking pans

◆ Rags or paper towels

◆ Wax paper or butcher paper

**Pans:** Two large, disposable aluminum baking pans are needed to stain larger pieces that will not fit directly into a can of stain.

**Rags or paper towels and wax paper or butcher paper:** Always have lots of rags or paper towels on hand for wiping excess stain off pieces and for cleaning up your work area. You may also want to put old rags, wax paper, or butcher paper on your work surface to protect it from the stain. **Caution:** Oily rags can be at risk for spontaneous combustion. Be sure to follow the manufacturer's suggestions on proper disposal of any rags used in conjunction with these types of products.

# AN OVERVIEW OF THE PROCESS

Understanding the entire process before you begin to cut relief portraits is the key to creating a beautifully executed end product. In this section, you'll find an overview of the process itself, plus some valuable information on improving your scrolling technique.

**Working in Relief.** Raising or lowering areas of a pattern gives a project greater depth and makes the final piece more realistic.

## UNDERSTANDING RELIEF

You may think relief is a difficult concept to understand, but once you learn the basic principles, you'll see that creating an animal in relief is a fairly easy idea to grasp.

Relief mimics nature, but it does so in a much tighter scale. Imagine being able to take the face of an animal—a wolf, for example—and compress it. Put one hand over the imaginary wolf's face and the other hand on the back of its head. As you bring your hands together, the wolf's nose, its mouth, its eyes, its ears, and its head all collapse under your hands. But they don't collapse completely flat. The nose still stands out farther than any other part of the head; the eyes still sink back; and the ears are now at the very back of the head. This is relief.

As a rule of thumb, the nose is the highest reference point when creating animals in relief. Everything else falls back gradually from that point when the animal is viewed from the front. Keep this concept in mind as you are working with the patterns and cutting the pieces.

## WORKING WITH PATTERNS

Many of the patterns in this book need to be enlarged to create the finished projects at the sizes shown. Of course, this is just a suggestion. The pattern can be cut as is or even smaller, depending on your skill as a scroller. Use a photocopier or a computer to change the size of the pattern.

The patterns in this book can also be altered to suit your scrolling skills. By deleting some cuts or slightly altering others, you can change the level of difficulty of a pattern, making it easier to scroll.

Before gluing the pattern down, use scissors to trim the pattern to within a half-inch of the outside border before affixing it to the wood. This cuts down on the amount of spray adhesive you need to use and will make it easier to trim the wood down to size.

Glue the pattern to the wood by applying temporary bond spray adhesive to the back of the pattern. Do not apply adhesive to the wood. The bond will be too strong if glue is applied to the pattern and the wood. Too much glue may also cause the stain to absorb unevenly into the wood.

If you find that you applied too much spray adhesive to the pattern and have difficulty removing it from the segments, simply use a small brush to apply a light coat of mineral spirits to the paper remaining on the segments. This will release the glue and the pattern can be removed easily.

**Cut the Pattern to Size.** Trim around the pattern before affixing it to the wood.

**Glue the Pattern to the Wood.** Spray temporary bond adhesive on the back of the pattern only.

**Remove Stuck-On Patterns.** Mineral spirits can help to remove stuck-on pattern paper.

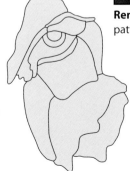

**Altering the Pattern.** Smoothing out pieces, like the ones that make up this wolf's eye area, can make a pattern easier to scroll.

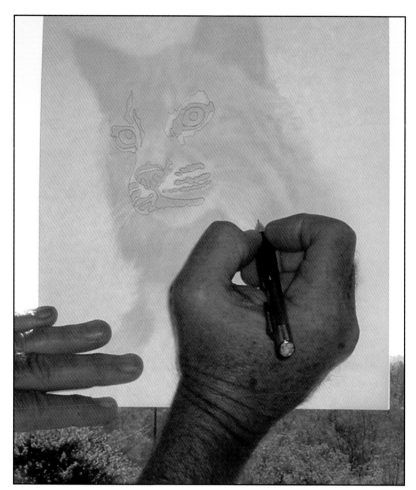

**Trace the Image.** Use a window or a light box to capture the distinguishing features of your subject.

## DEVELOPING CUSTOM PATTERNS

If, like me, you enjoy creating realistic portraits, you will eventually want to do an original project of your own design. Almost everyone has a favorite subject that he or she would like to reproduce as an original pattern, and you do not have to be an accomplished artist to create a pattern. There really is no magic involved, and no expensive array of equipment is required (computers are nice but not necessary). Every pattern in this book was developed using the simple steps I've outlined here.

**First, you will need a photograph of your intended subject.** On the Internet, there is a wealth of free photo downloads available for almost any subject you can imagine. Or you can try using your own photographs. The procedure is essentially the same for downloaded or hard copy photographs, except that if I'm using a hard copy photograph I scan it into my computer, crop the portion of the image I want to reproduce in the pattern, and resize the image to about 8" x 10". Then, I print the image in black and white on plain letter paper.

**Second, trace over the image.** You will need a pad of 9" x 12" tracing paper, a thin lead mechanical pencil, and a roll of clear tape. Place a sheet of tracing paper over your black-and-white photo and tape the two top corners of the tracing paper to the top corners of the photo.

Find a suitable window that catches good sunlight. (If you happen to have a light box, you can use it instead of a window.) Tape the top corners of the assembled photo and tracing paper to the window. Don't tape all four corners down because you will want to be able to lift the tracing paper up to see the photo from time to time. Trace the photo onto the tracing paper as a line drawing.

As you complete projects in this book and become familiar with how the patterns are composed, you will have a better feel for what you need in your drawing. Don't attempt to capture every detail. On most photos, a lot of detail will be obscured by shadow or subtle changes in shading, and you won't be able to see it through the tracing paper. You only want sufficient detail to convey realism in the image.

### Using Computer Programs to Trace an Image

Computer programs can be of considerable aid when making some patterns, but they can be virtually useless on others. The computer can only capture detail it can "see" in a photo. As a result, when trying to electronically convert a photo to a line drawing, subtle changes in color values often do not suggest a line that the computer can identify as such. In those cases, you can often achieve some very respectable results by combining the computer's capabilities with your own drawing skills.

Too much detail, in my opinion, results in the finished product appearing too "busy" and really adds nothing but unnecessary work to the project.

**Third, join the lines in the tracing to create segments**. When the tracing is complete, take the photo down and separate it from the tracing paper. Using the photo as a guide and drawing freehand, join your lines in the tracing to make segments. Avoid creating straight lines, since there are few straight lines in nature and they will detract from the natural flow of the overall pattern. Make sure all of the segments are closed. In other words, there can be no dead-end lines inside the pattern. Think of it as creating pieces for a jigsaw puzzle that will be cut out and then reassembled into a whole picture.

**Finally, enlarge the pattern on a copy machine to the desired dimensions.** If you want thinner lines, trace over your pencil lines with a fine-tipped pen. Give the ink a couple of hours to dry and then, using a soft white drafting eraser, carefully erase what remains of the thicker pencil lines. Retain the original photo to use as a color reference when staining.

Keep your first few patterns simple. At first, try to limit the number of segments, and don't incorporate too much detail into the image. It's much like learning to use the scroll saw. The more you do it, the more your skills develop, and the happier you will be with the results.

## Making Adjustments to Your Patterns

One word of caution when you are drawing your own patterns—or altering prepared patterns: Sometimes you will find that they don't always turn out as anticipated. On occasion, you may need to make in-process adjustments to the pattern to make the finished piece look like you intended it to look. *The White-Tailed Buck* project on page 73 is a good example. After I had finished cutting and staining this project, I discovered a couple of changes I needed to make in the pattern for the finished piece to be more pleasing to the eye. Rather than start all over, I decided to incorporate the changes into the project. These kinds of changes are to be expected, and, with a little creativity, you can solve the problem without scrapping your entire project.

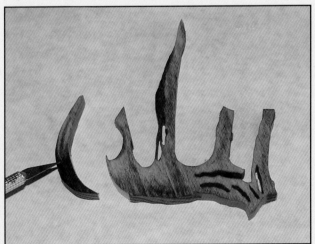

After I stained the antler on the buck, I decided to put more relief and realism into the deer's right antler. Originally, just a dark walnut stain shadowed the curve. I went back to the saw and cut the tip off so I could elevate it in relief.

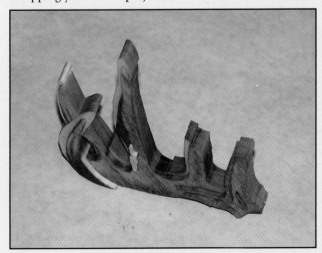

After I glued the pieces, I noticed that some unstained wood was revealed at the joint, making it necessary for me to do some additional staining in order to "fix" the project.

# CUTTING THE PROJECTS

Virtually anyone with some experience on the scroll saw is capable of cutting the patterns in this book. However, if you are a beginner, I highly recommend John Nelson's *Scroll Saw Workbook*. A little time spent on the exercises in that book will enable you to become much more proficient on your saw and much more confident in your skills when faced with what might appear to be a complicated pattern. I also recommend that you review each project before starting in order to familiarize yourself with each step in the overall process.

All of the patterns in this book are cut using continuous cuts within the pattern. There is no waste wood, as with fretwork. For some patterns, you may need to plan your cuts before you begin so you don't find yourself left with pieces that are too small to cut. Always cut the smaller pieces off the larger pieces first.

Some patterns require that blade entry holes be drilled for inside cuts to create segments for spots or eyes. Use the smallest bit possible that will allow the selected blade to pass through the hole.

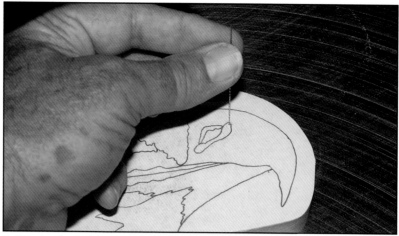

**Drill holes for Inside Cuts.** Blade entry holes, made with a drill, allow the scroll saw blade to be threaded into areas where interior cuts are needed.

## STAINING

Assemble all of your materials for staining in one area. You will need the brushes, black permanent marker, rags or paper towels, and aluminum tins that we discussed in Part 1, "Basic Equipment," page 1. The stains used for the projects in this book are golden oak, dark walnut, and colonial maple.

The majority of the projects are stained with only two colors of stain: golden oak and dark walnut. These colors are smear mixed directly on the segment to create highlights and to blend lighter shades into darker shades.

Although only two colors of stain are the primary colors used, I frequently incorporate colonial maple stain to achieve reddish-orange colors and highlights such as those found in foxes and some of the big jungle cats. Colonial maple may be smear mixed with golden oak for excellent results.

Prepare the staining area by laying down some absorbent material, like paper towels, on which the stained segments can be placed. I usually tape some paper towels over butcher paper to prevent the stain from bleeding through onto my worktable. Be sure to move any project pieces that remain unstained away from the staining area.

There are three staining techniques employed in these projects: dipping, smear mixing, and slosh staining. Dipping typically

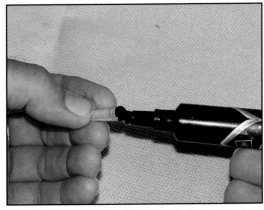

**Creating Dark Shades.** Get a very dark shade by first coloring the piece with a black permanent marker then dipping it in the stain.

involves small pieces that can be dipped directly into the can of stain. This technique often produces one color. Smear-mixed pieces are first dipped or slosh stained. Then, while the piece is still wet, a brush, or similar instrument, is used to smear, or blend, another color into the first. Slosh staining is a technique employed for pieces too large to dip—simply pour stain into a disposable aluminum baking pan, place the piece in the pan, and tilt it until the piece has been covered. Though it wastes a lot of stain, it is the only way to evenly stain larger pieces.

If a very black color is desired, simply color the surface with a black permanent marker, and then stain it dark walnut. If a very light shade is required, stain the piece with golden oak and then immediately wipe it back off. White areas are left unstained. Of course, some wood species absorb stain more readily than others. Practice staining on a scrap of the wood you intended to use in the project to get the best results.

Keep in mind that there are no hard-and-fast rules when it comes to staining these projects. Individual creativity and artistic license are what make them unique. I encourage you to experiment with any shades of stain you feel might be suitable for a given project. Get your artistic juices flowing and create a masterpiece!

**Preparing the Staining Area.** Tape several layers of paper towels over butcher paper to absorb excess stain and to protect your work area. A variety of brushes and several colors of stain are needed for the projects.

# THREE BASIC STAINING TECHNIQUES

**Dipping:** Most of the project pieces are small enough that they can be held with small tongs or pliers and be dipped directly into the can of stain. Allow the excess stain to drip from the pieces; then, move them to the prepared surface to dry.

**Smear mixing:** This technique involves one base stain and one or more stains for highlight or shadow. This method is generally accomplished by first staining the segment golden oak (using the dipping or slosh staining method) and then, while the piece is still wet, smearing dark walnut onto the golden oak to achieve the desired effect. A finger, a small artist's brush, or a cotton swab may be used effectively for this purpose. Allow the piece to dry completely on the prepared surface.

**Slosh staining:** I use slosh staining only on pieces that are too large to dip. Simply pour enough stain into a disposable aluminum baking pan to coat the bottom of the pan. Then, put the piece in and tilt the pan until the piece has been covered. Remove the piece from the stain with tongs and set it on the prepared surface to dry. Slosh staining wastes a lot of stain (unless you can pour it back into the can), but it is the quickest way to evenly stain larger pieces.

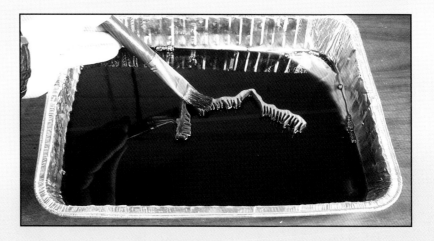

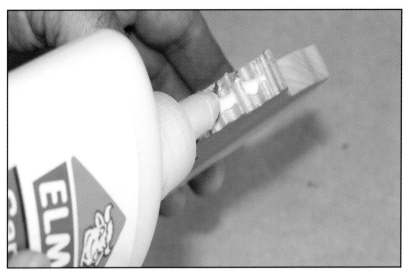

**Adding Strength with Glue.** Wood glue lends strength to joints but takes time to dry.

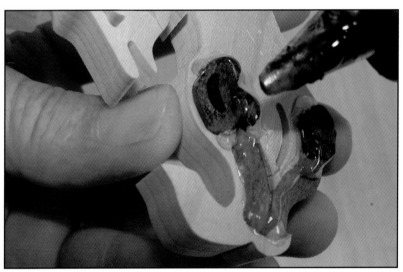

**Using Hot Glue.** Hot glue dries quickly and holds the relief pieces in place.

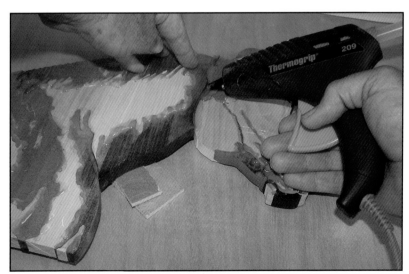

**Shims for Assembly.** Shims are small pieces of ⅛" plywood placed between the segment and the worktable that keep the segment at the desired elevation until the glue sets up.

## GLUING

The accepted method for gluing pieces together has been to use common wood glue. I didn't like this method because of the time required for the glue to set and the fact that the glue runs through the saw kerfs onto the face of my work. The purpose of the glue in this segmented relief portraiture is not intended strictly for structural integrity (additional structural support is provided when the portrait is attached to the backer), so I use hot glue, and lots of it.

Hot glue is unconventional but an excellent choice. Its quick drying time allows you to set a piece to the proper relief height, glue it in place, and then move almost immediately to the next piece. However, hot glue is not used exclusively.

I will occasionally use wood glue to adhere small segments to the outer edges of a portrait or when the seams between the pieces do not interlock, such as those in a deer's antlers. In these cases, there is little support where the segments attach to the rest of the portrait. The chemical make-up of wood glue will add strength to the wood, create a stronger joint, and give you a stronger finished project. Additionally, I will use silicon glue to attach my finished portraits to their backings.

Before gluing the segments, always ensure that the stain has completely dried before starting the glue-up phase of the project. Depending on heat and humidity, drying time can take from several hours to a couple of days. Then, dry fit the segments back together on a layout board made from heavy cardboard or luan. This makes gluing the project a lot easier because all of the segments will be in the order you want them.

Gluing the segments in the portrait is another opportunity for artistic expression. Again, there are no hard-and-fast rules, just a few suggestions. The goal is a three-dimensional effect when the portrait is viewed from a distance.

Glue the segments higher or lower in relation to each other to mimic relief in a live subject. Areas that suggest shadow would be set back, while areas that suggest light reflection would be raised. For example, when facing you, a wolf's nose is closer to you than his ears are. Accordingly, you would raise the nose higher in relief than the rest of the wolf's head. The eyes would be set slightly back.

## SHIMS

Shims are simply small pieces of ⅛-inch plywood that are placed under a segment in a large portrait when gluing it up. The shim is temporarily placed between the segment and the worktable to keep the segment at the desired elevation until the glue sets up. I only use them when a project is so large as to become cumbersome when trying to hold the segment in place by hand. Once the glue is dry, I remove the shim from behind the project.

### The Flip Side

Here's a trick to flipping or moving projects with lots of pieces. With projects, such as *The Giraffe* project on page 77 or *The Jaguar* on page 89, that have lots of small pieces easily displaced during a move, I dry fit the project on a piece of luan or stiff cardboard. The backing makes it easier to move the project to another area of my workshop without shifting the pieces.

Also, when projects have many small pieces, I like to glue them up from the back. The luan or stiff cardboard helps me flip the project efficiently. I simply dry fit the project on the cardboard, sandwich the project between another piece of stiff cardboard, press the two pieces of cardboard tightly together between the palms of my hands, then flip the entire assembly. Now the project is ready to be glued from the back, and all of the pieces are still in perfect order.

**1**

Dry fit the pieces on a piece of luan.

**2**

Place another piece of luan on top of the project.

**3**

Press the boards together between the palms of your hands and invert.

## CONSTRUCTING CUSTOM FRAMES

Displaying your completed project in a nice frame that complements the piece is as important as doing a good job on the piece itself. You can buy frames custom built for your work, but they are expensive. Another option is to check yard sales and flea markets for inexpensive pictures that are mounted in nice frames. Discard the picture and use the frame. The best option, however, is to build your own frame.

I use trim called false tread molding to build my frames. It is used for making false fronts on stair treads and is perfect for these projects because of the deep frame and pleasing profile. I buy it in poplar because of the reasonable price and the fact that I can stain it to look like expensive hardwood. For an example of building a custom frame, let's look at *The Bobcat*, found on page 93.

The first step in building a frame is to determine the size of backer you'll need. I like to frame my work so that, when centered in the frame, there is as much vacant space from the top of the image to the inside top edge of the frame as there is from the bottom of the image to the inside bottom edge of the frame. The same applies to the sides.

I generally estimate how much vacant space I want based on the size of the image. Because of the size of *The Bobcat*, I'll go with about 1½ inches on all four sides. The longest dimension of *The Bobcat* is 13 inches. I need 1½ inches at both the top and the bottom, so the length of the exposed backer will be 16 inches. The widest part of the image is 10 inches, so the width will be 13 inches.

**1**

Choose false tread molding to make your own custom frames. You will notice that false tread molding has a ¼" groove cut throughout its length.

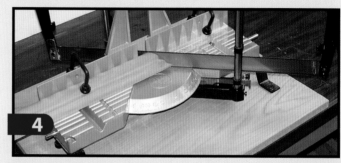

**4**

Miter the corners to 45-degree angles, taking care to maintain the exact original length of each of the four sides. I want the depth of the frame to be prevalent on the inside, so I cut the miters accordingly.

**7**

Remove the frame clamp and apply wood glue sparingly to the face of the corner cuts.

**10**

Stain the backer. I used colonial maple with this piece to pick up the color in *The Bobcat*'s nose and the highlights in the ears.

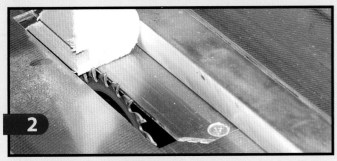

**2**

Remove the outside of the groove with a table saw to create a rabbet that the picture will nest in when the frame is assembled. Use a scrap piece of molding to adjust your table saw fence and blade height.

**3**

When cut, the rabbet will measure $\frac{7}{16}$". Add two times the width of the rabbet to both the length and the width of the backer. Accordingly the backer will be 13$\frac{7}{8}$" x 16$\frac{7}{8}$", but don't cut the backer out until the frame has been assembled. Add two times the width of the molding to the exposed length of the picture to determine the length of the sides of the frame. Cut the two sides exactly 19$\frac{5}{8}$" long and the top and bottom exactly 16$\frac{5}{8}$" long.

**5**

Carefully sand the small burrs left by the saw and dry fit the frame in the clamps.

**6**

Check that the corner joints are tight.

**8**

Reclamp the frame, making sure no glue squeezes out onto the face of the frame. After the glue has dried for several hours, remove the clamps and use two 1" brads to secure each corner.

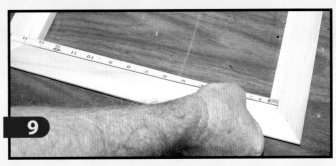

**9**

Flip the frame over and measure the length and width inside the rabbets. Then, cut the backer to fit.

**11**

The completed frame and backer. The frame was stained dark walnut to complement the dark areas of the cat.

**12**

These three frames are examples of what can be achieved with different colors of stains on poplar molding. The top one was stained with golden oak, the middle with dark walnut, and the bottom with red mahogany.

# STEP-BY-STEP
# DEMONSTRATIONS

These first three projects were designed to familiarize you with the steps and practices involved in segmented portraiture and to provide "hands on" experience before progressing to the larger, more complex projects. They each consist of just a few segments that are fairly large and are not difficult to cut out.

Each project includes a number of different guides to help you through the process. The objective focuses on the most important skill of the piece. A recommended cutting order is provided to help you learn to plan your cuts. Using this tool will help you limit the number of blade entry holes you must drill to get to inner pieces and will ensure that you have enough to hold on to as you scroll smaller pieces. The staining and assembly charts provide the general staining and assembly steps that were used to complete the piece. It is important to note that these charts are simply a starting point for the projects. Be sure to use the full-page photo of the finished project and to modify the staining colors and assembly levels to suit your personal tastes.

When these three projects have been completed, you will have developed the basic skills required to move on to the more complex projects and to better understand the art form as a whole.

# THE BISON SKULL

**Objective:** Learn how individual pieces, when glued in relief, can add realism to a scrolled portrait.

The bison is the largest terrestrial animal in North America. Until the 19th century, as many as 60 million bison, or buffalo, lived on the Great Plains from Mexico into Canada. From 1830 until 1889, methodical destruction by settlers, for sport and for hides, reduced this number to less than 1,000. The remaining bones that littered the plains were then collected and shipped east of the Mississippi to be ground into fertilizer. Today well over 200,000 bison live in protected areas and on private ranches.

The first project in this book is a tribute to this majestic beast. Enlarge the pattern for *The Bison Skull* at least 135%; however, you can make it larger if you desire. The procedure for creating this piece is the same regardless of its final size. It is a fairly simple pattern and can be cut and stained in just a few hours.

## Tools and Materials

- Light-colored, soft wood of choice (poplar), ½" to ¾" thick, sized to fit the pattern
- Scroll saw
- #5 reverse skip-tooth blades for general cuts
- #2 reverse skip-tooth blades for intricate cuts
- Temporary bond spray adhesive
- Drill or drill press
- ⅟₁₆" drill bit
- Sandpaper, small square of 120 grit
- Wax paper or butcher paper, large sheet
- Paper towels, one roll, or rags
- Small tongs or pliers
- Golden oak stain, one 32 oz. can
- Dark walnut stain, one 32 oz. can
- Brushes, small and medium
- Hot glue gun
- Glue sticks
- Wood glue, small bottle

## CUTTING ORDER

Start by cutting the outside edge of the bison skull; then, cut the centerline through the skull to divide the project into two parts. Cut the left-side segments; then, cut the right-side segments.

**1** Outside edge
**2** Centerline through skull
**3** Left-side segments
    Horn
    Forehead
    Forehead crease
    Eye socket
    Bridge of nose
    Inside of nose

**4** Right-side segments
    Horn
    Forehead
    Forehead crease
    Eye socket
    Bridge of nose
    Inside of nose

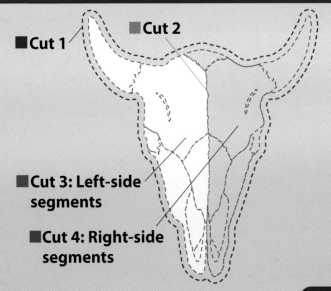

■Cut 1    ■Cut 2

■Cut 3: Left-side segments

■Cut 4: Right-side segments

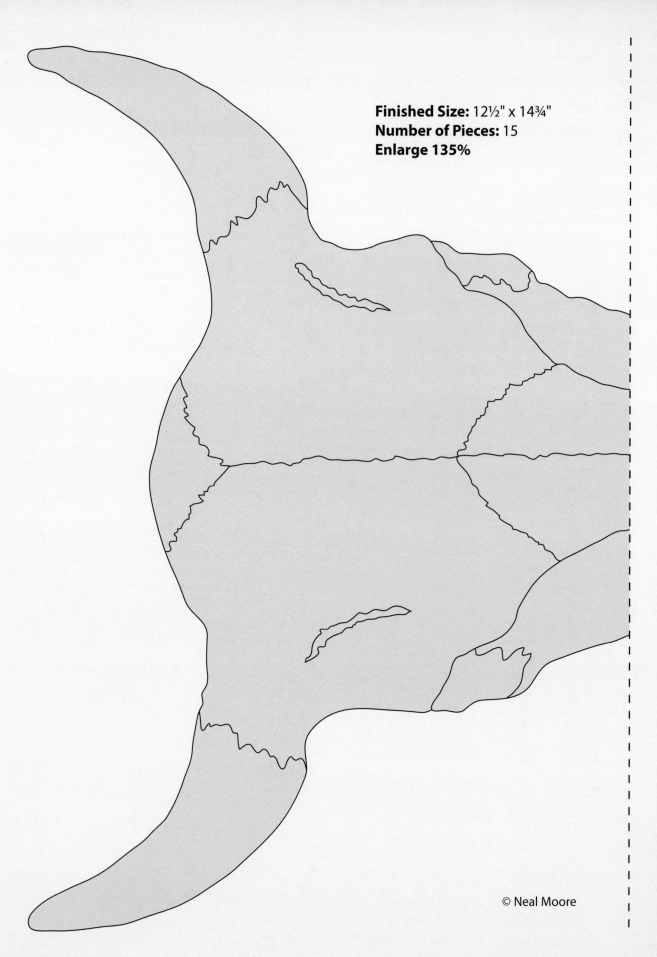

**Finished Size:** 12½" x 14¾"
**Number of Pieces:** 15
**Enlarge 135%**

© Neal Moore

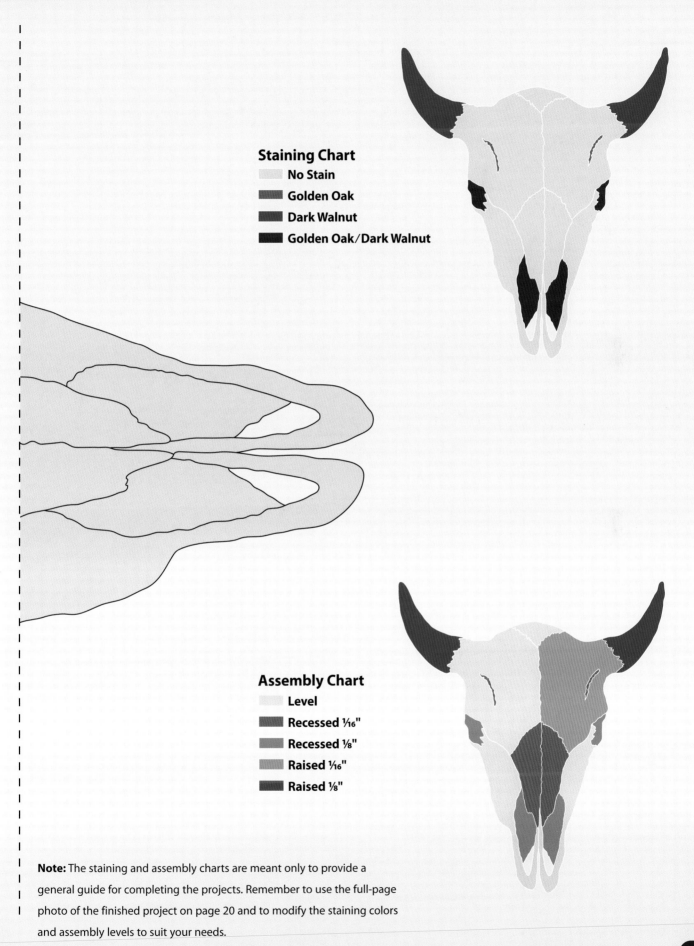

**Staining Chart**

No Stain
Golden Oak
Dark Walnut
Golden Oak/Dark Walnut

**Assembly Chart**

Level
Recessed ¹⁄₁₆"
Recessed ⅛"
Raised ¹⁄₁₆"
Raised ⅛"

**Note:** The staining and assembly charts are meant only to provide a general guide for completing the projects. Remember to use the full-page photo of the finished project on page 20 and to modify the staining colors and assembly levels to suit your needs.

## CUTTING THE PATTERN

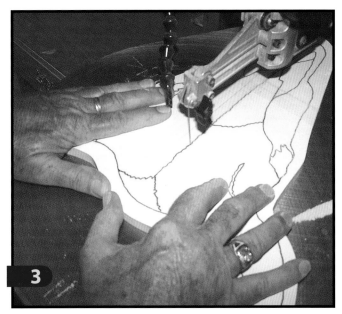

**1**

Use scissors to trim the pattern to within ½" of the outside border. Then, apply the pattern to the wood with temporary bond spray adhesive. Take care to smooth out any air bubbles between the pattern and the wood.

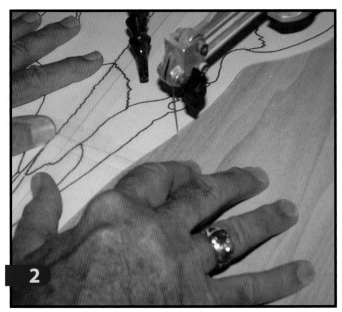

**2**

Next, using a #5 reverse skip-tooth blade, cut around the pattern using the ½" margin as a guide. This makes the remaining work more manageable on the saw table.

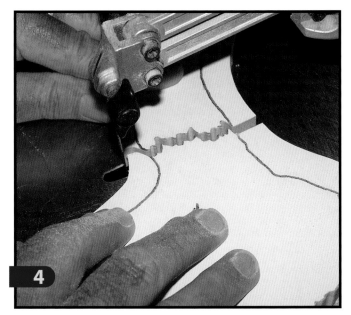

**3**

Now, following the pattern line that runs vertically through the center of the skull, cut the pattern into two pieces.

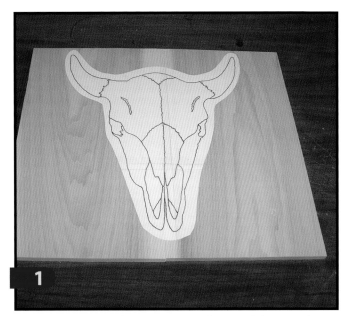

**4**

Put the right-hand half of the project aside, and start cutting segments from the left-hand side. Remove the horn first.

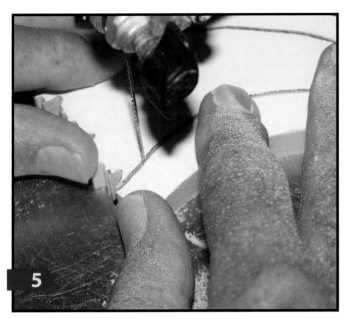

**5**

Cut around the horn on the pattern line, removing the margin.

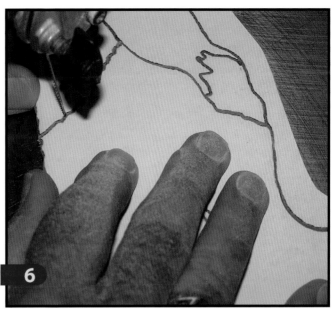

**6**

Next, cut out the segment that represents the left side of the forehead.

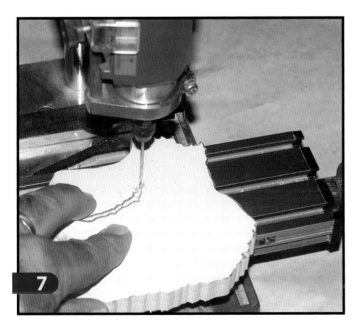

**7**

At this point, select a drill bit sized for a #5 blade. Just inside the crease in the forehead, drill a blade entry hole. This hole should touch the pattern line.

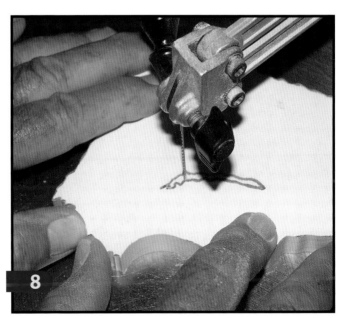

**8**

Using a piece of sandpaper, lightly hand sand the burr from the back of the drilled hole and thread the blade through the blade entry hole. Cut out the segment, taking care to exit the blade through the center of the hole. Be sure to remove all of the segments as you cut them.

## CUTTING THE PATTERN

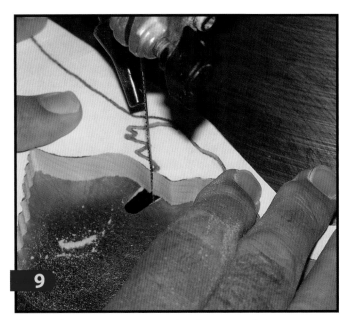

**9**

Cut out the segment representing the eye socket.

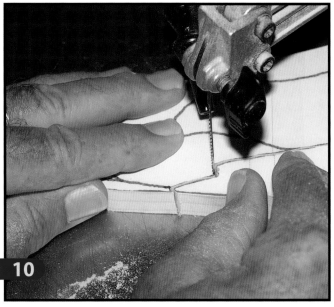

**10**

Cut the segment for the bridge of the nose.

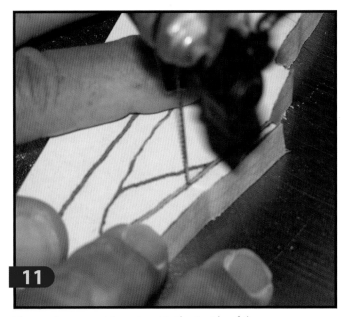

**11**

The next segment to cut out is the inside of the nose.

**12**

Then, cut off and discard the bottom part of that segment.

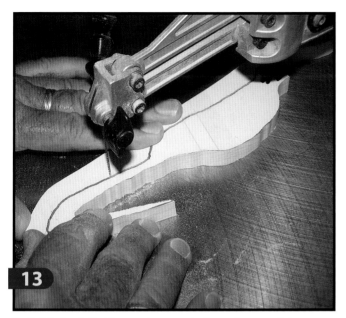

**13**

To finish the left side, cut the margin from the remaining segment, and gently remove the pattern from all the segments you have cut thus far.

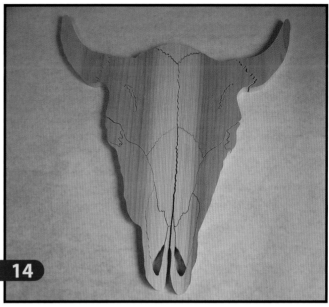

**14**

Cut the right side of the pattern in the same manner as the left side. Assemble the segments, but do not glue any segments at this point.

## STAINING THE PIECES

**15**

Start by dipping each horn in dark walnut stain. Use tongs or pliers to remove the pieces from the stain, and lay them face up on several layers of paper towels to dry. Use the staining chart on page 23 and the full-page photo on page 20 to aid you as you stain the project.

**16**

Dip the two creases from each side of the forehead in golden oak stain and allow them to dry face up on the paper towels.

## STAINING THE PIECES

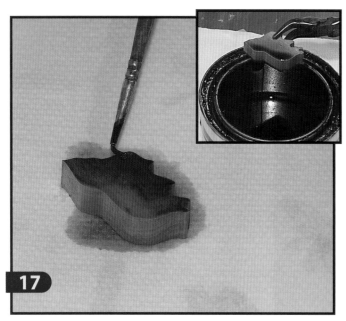

17

Stain the segments for the eye sockets with golden oak; then, while the stain is still wet, use a small brush to smear mix dark walnut onto the inside edge, creating a shadow.

18

Dip the segments representing the inside of the nose in golden oak stain and smear mix the edges with dark walnut stain. Place these segments on the towels to dry.

## ASSEMBLING THE PROJECT

19

After the stain has dried completely (this may take several days), reassemble the project in preparation for gluing it up.

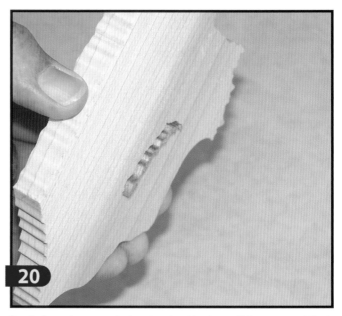

20

Begin by using wood glue to glue the long, thin segment that represents the crease in the left side of the skull. Push it back so it is recessed about ¹⁄₁₆". As you go through the assembly process, refer to the assembly chart on page 23 for additional information.

**21**

Now, on the back side, run a fillet of hot glue completely around the segment, bonding it in place. Wait until the glue has hardened, and then glue the right side in the same manner.

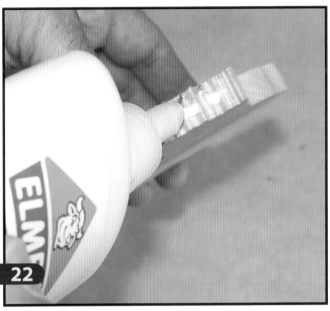

**22**

Next, on the left side, apply a few drops of wood glue to the edge of the skull where the horn joins that segment. Glue the horn to the segment so it is raised about ⅛" when viewed from the front.

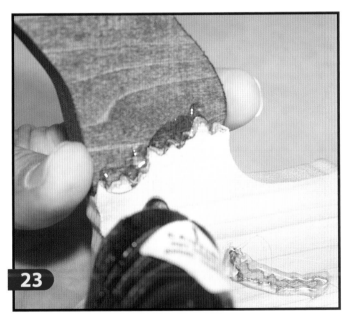

**23**

Run a bead of hot glue along the joint on the back side to hold the pieces together while the wood glue dries. Glue together the horn, skull, and crease on the right side in the same manner using both hot glue and wood glue. Notice that wood glue is used to join the horn to the segment because there are no interlocking segments to add structural integrity.

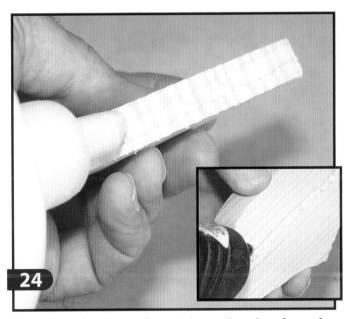

**24**

Next, place a few drops of wood glue on the edge of one of the two center segments. Elevate the other segment about 1⁄16" to ensure the kerf will be visible, and run a bead of hot glue on the back of the joint between the two segments.

## ASSEMBLING THE PROJECT

**25**

Now, glue up the left jaw with hot glue. Push the dark segment in about ⅛" so it is recessed when viewed from the front, and run a good bead of hot glue over the joint on the back. Glue the right jaw in the same manner.

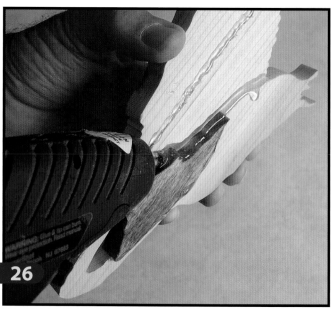

**26**

Next, hot glue the left jaw to the two center segments that were glued together previously. Elevate the center so it is about ⅛" higher than the jaw, and run a bead of glue over the joint.

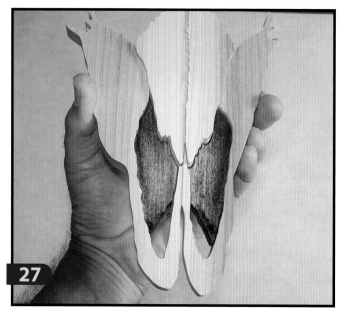

**27**

Now, fit the right jaw, much like a jigsaw puzzle, into the left side. These two pieces are flush: there is no height difference. Ensure the elevation on the right and left sides is the same, and run a bead of hot glue over the joints in the back.

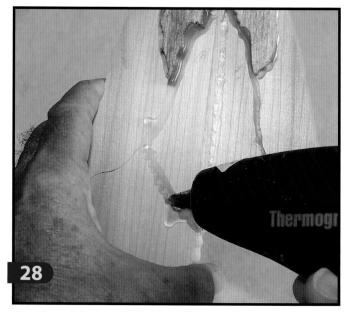

**28**

Next, hot glue the right forehead and horn in place by running a bead of glue over the joint on the back. Hot glue the left forehead and horn in place in the same manner; then, hot glue the top of the skull.

**29**

Recess the dark segments representing the eye sockets about ⅛" in the skull and hot glue them in place.

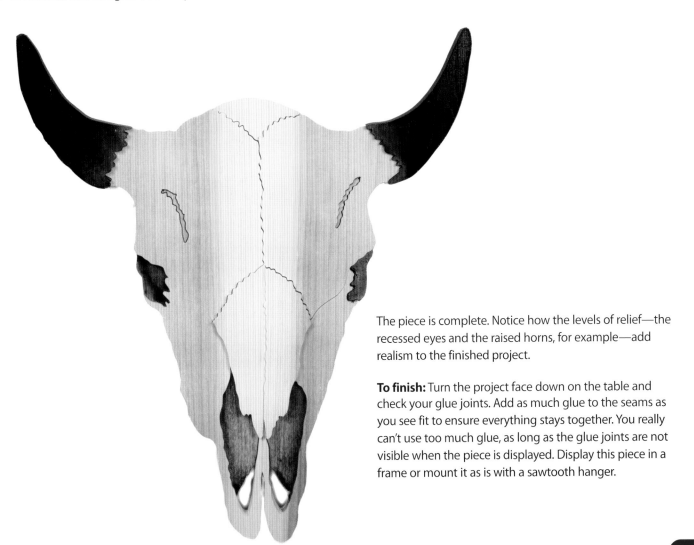

The piece is complete. Notice how the levels of relief—the recessed eyes and the raised horns, for example—add realism to the finished project.

**To finish:** Turn the project face down on the table and check your glue joints. Add as much glue to the seams as you see fit to ensure everything stays together. You really can't use too much glue, as long as the glue joints are not visible when the piece is displayed. Display this piece in a frame or mount it as is with a sawtooth hanger.

# THE EAGLE

## Objective: Learn to study patterns and plan your cuts accordingly.

The American bald eagle was designated the national bird of the United States in 1782. Its name does not imply a lack of feathers but instead is derived from the word "piebald," meaning "marked with white." The bald eagle reigns as the second largest bird of prey in North America, second only to the California condor.

The Eagle is an easy project consisting of only 13 segments. I sized this pattern to 100% and cut it from ½" poplar using a #5 reverse skip-tooth blade. I don't like to use precision-ground blades for portraits because I find them too aggressive for this type of cutting; however, I used one for part of this project so the blade would be more visible in the photographs.

### Tools and Materials

- ◆ Light-colored, soft wood of choice (poplar), ½" to ¾" thick, sized to fit the pattern
- ◆ Scroll saw
- ◆ #5 reverse skip-tooth scroll saw blades
- ◆ #2 reverse skip-tooth blades for intricate cuts
- ◆ Temporary bond spray adhesive
- ◆ Drill or drill press
- ◆ ¹⁄₁₆" drill bit
- ◆ Sandpaper, small square of 120 grit
- ◆ Wax paper or butcher paper, large sheet
- ◆ Paper towels, one roll, or rags
- ◆ Small tongs or pliers
- ◆ Golden oak stain, one 32 oz. can
- ◆ Dark walnut stain, one 32 oz. can
- ◆ Colonial maple stain, one 32 oz. can
- ◆ Brushes, small and medium
- ◆ Black permanent marker
- ◆ White acrylic paint or gesso
- ◆ Hot glue gun
- ◆ Glue sticks

## CUTTING ORDER

Before you cut this pattern, you'll want to plan several cuts so you don't "cut yourself into a corner." **Planned Cut #1:** The eye. You'll need a blade entry hole to cut those interior pieces. The best place to position the blade entry hole is at the top of the eyeball (see Step 2) so you can cut the center piece first. The remaining cuts for the eye do not need blade entry holes. **Planned Cut #2:** The nostril. You'll need to cut three interior pieces, but with careful planning, you'll only need to drill one blade entry hole. Position it at the outer edge of the nostril (see Step 3). **Planned Cut #3:** The beak and crown. The final cut is a continuous cut over the eye, down the back of the head, and over the top of the head, back to the starting point. This cut was planned to ensure a sharp point on the beak and to provide access to the eye segments later on (see Step 5).

Once you have these key cuts planned, the complete cutting order for your project should begin with cutting the outside edge of The Eagle pattern first. Move to the nostril segments, then the crown and beak. Finish cutting the beak. Cut the eye. Then, finish all remaining cuts.

1 Outside edge
2 Nostril segments
3 Crown and beak
4 Eye
5 All remaining cuts

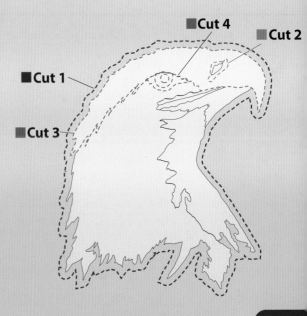

**Finished Size:** 7" x 8½"
**Number of Pieces:** 13

© Neal Moore

## Staining Chart
- No Stain
- Golden Oak
- Dark Walnut
- Black Marker/Dark Walnut
- Golden Oak/Dark Walnut
- Golden Oak/Colonial Maple

## Assembly Chart
- Level
- Recessed 1/16"
- Raised 1/16"
- Raised 1/8"
- Raised 3/16"
- Raised 1/4"

**Note:** The staining and assembly charts are meant only to provide a general guide for completing the projects. Remember to use the full-page photo of the finished project on page 32 and to modify the staining colors and assembly levels to suit your needs.

## CUTTING THE PATTERN

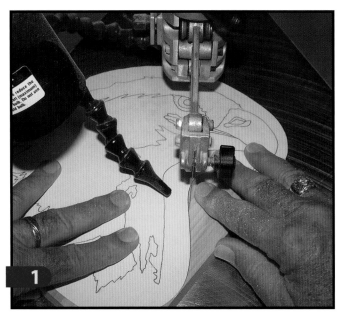

**1**

Trim the pattern, leaving about a ½" margin all around, and affix the pattern to the wood with a light coat of temporary bond spray adhesive. Trim the excess wood from around the pattern using the paper margin as a guide.

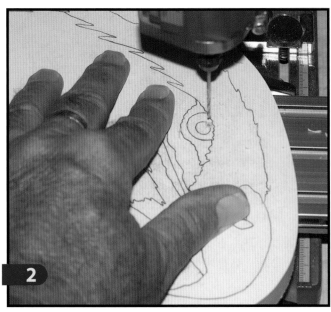

**2**

At this point, drill a blade entry hole for the eye. Using a bit sized for a #5 blade, drill the blade entry hole for the eye just inside the pupil and touching the pattern line.

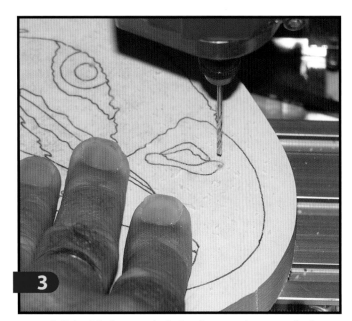

**3**

Now, drill the blade entry hole for the nostril just inside the farthest point and touching the line.

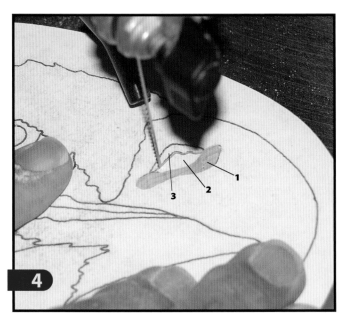

**4**

Feed the blade through the hole in the nostril. The nostril is made up of three segments. Cut them in the order shown in the photograph. Remove the pieces once they are cut.

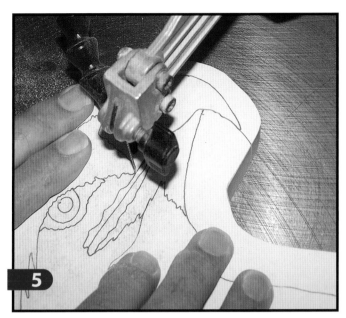

**5**

Now, starting the cut in the margin under the eagle's beak, make one continuous cut following the pattern line that goes over the eye and down the back of the head. Continue this cut over the top of the head and exit at the tip of the beak where you started.

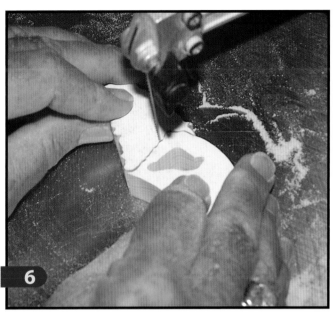

**6**

Cut on the line starting at the top of the beak and separate it from the head.

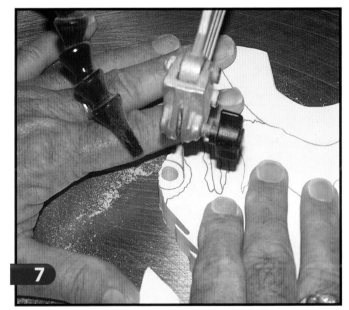

**7**

Thread the blade through the blade entry hole in the eye and cut out the pupil. Then, cut the eye segments in the order shown on the photograph.

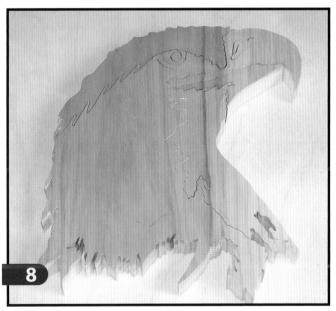

**8**

The remaining cuts are simple and require no explanation. Finish cutting the pattern, remove the paper from the segments, and assemble the project for staining.

## STAINING THE PIECES

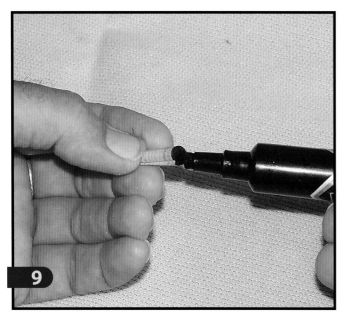

9

First, color the pupil of the eye with a black permanent marker. Use the staining chart on page 35 and the full-page photo on page 32 to aid you as you stain the project.

10

Then, dip the segment in dark walnut stain and place it aside to dry. Stain the center of the nostril the same way.

11

Next, dip the beak in golden oak stain.

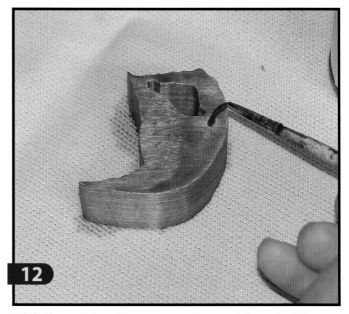

12

While the stain is still wet, smear mix colonial maple stain on the upper third of the beak for highlight.

13

Dip the eye in golden oak stain and place it aside to dry.

14

Dip the remaining eye segment in dark walnut stain and place it aside to dry.

15

Dip the lower part of the beak in golden oak stain, and, while the stain is still wet, smear mix dark walnut stain along the upper edge for shadow.

16

The last segment to be stained is the largest segment. It is stained golden oak. Simply brush the stain on to avoid unnecessary mess and waste of stain. The remaining segments are left unstained.

## STAINING THE PIECES

**17**

When the stain has thoroughly dried, assemble the project, and paint the small white highlight dot in the eye with white acrylic paint or gesso. You are now ready to glue up the project.

## ASSEMBLING THE PROJECT

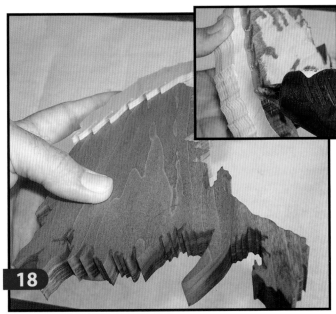

**18**

First, hold the lighter segment of the head elevated about ⅛", and then run a bead of glue over the joint on the back. As you go through the assembly process, remember to refer to the assembly chart on page 35 for additional information.

**19**

Next, recess the pupil in the eye about ¹⁄₁₆" and glue it in from the back.

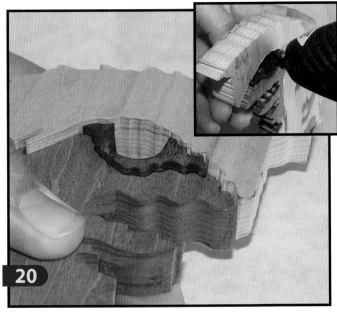

**20**

Now, position the dark walnut eye segment so it is recessed about ¹⁄₁₆" below the top of the head and elevated about ¹⁄₁₆" above the lower portion of the head. Glue it in place on the back side.

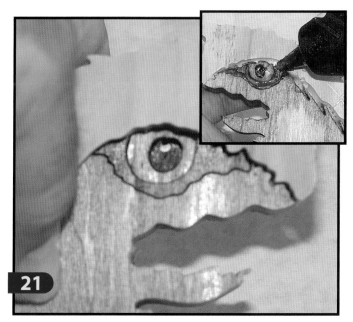

**21**

Position the eyeball so it is slightly recessed and glue it in place on the back side.

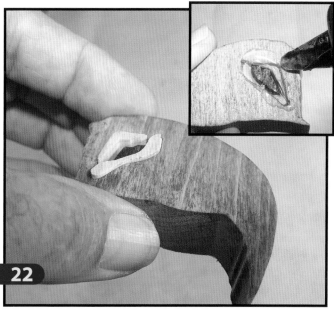

**22**

Position the three nostril segments so the lighter segments are raised slightly higher than the beak. Recess the dark center segment. Glue the three nostril segments in as one piece.

**23**

Fit the light throat segment and elevate it to the same level as the top of the head.

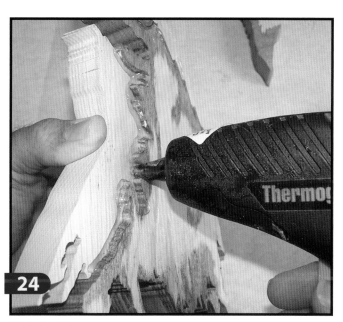

**24**

While holding the segment in place, glue it up.

## ASSEMBLING THE PROJECT

**25**

Position the lower beak so it is flush with the lighter throat segment.

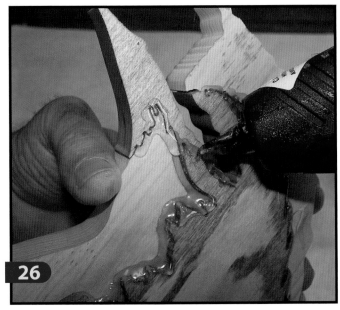

**26**

Glue the lower beak and the lighter throat segments.

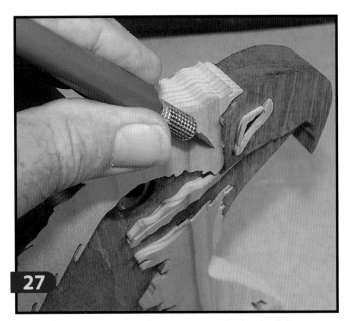

**27**

Insert the two segments that represent the back of the mouth. Position them so they are the same elevation as the top of the head. Then, insert the upper beak.

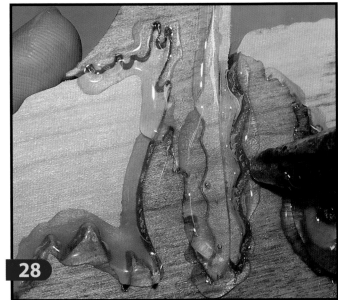

**28**

Glue in the pieces.

**29**

A low-angle photo shows the relief in the finished project.

The completed piece. Notice how our planned cuts affected the finished project—blade entry holes are limited and do not detract from the overall appearance and the point of the beak is sharp, as it would be on a live eagle.

**To finish:** *The Eagle* can be displayed mounted on a natural oval slab, framed, or displayed as is using a sawtooth hanger.

# THE WILD MUSTANG

**Objective:** Learn to divide large projects into manageable pieces and to blend stain for smooth transitions.

Wild mustangs are of domestic European ancestry. European settlers brought horses with them to North America, some of which escaped or were released into the wild. The word "mustang" is derived from the Spanish word *mestenos*, which means "strayed." Mustangs are found primarily in Mexico and on the western plains of the United States.

Here, we'll focus on dividing a large project into manageable pieces and blending stain for a smooth transition from one color to another. Enlarge the pattern to 130%. Although larger, *The Wild Mustang* is no more difficult than the two previous projects. Read through all steps of the project before starting in order to familiarize yourself with each step in the overall process.

## Tools and Materials

- Light-colored, soft wood of choice (poplar), ½" to ¾" thick, sized to fit the pattern
- Scroll saw
- #5 reverse skip-tooth blades for general cuts
- #2 reverse skip-tooth blades for intricate cuts
- Temporary bond spray adhesive
- Drill or drill press
- ¹⁄₁₆" drill bit
- Sandpaper, small square of 120 grit
- Wax paper or butcher paper, large sheet
- Paper towels, one roll, or rags
- Small tongs or pliers
- Golden oak stain, one 32oz. can
- Dark walnut stain, one 32 oz. can
- Colonial maple stain, one 32 oz. can
- Brushes, small and medium
- Black permanent marker
- Aluminum baking pans
- White acrylic paint or gesso
- Hot glue gun
- Glue sticks
- Wood glue, small bottle

## CUTTING ORDER

Begin by cutting the outside edge. Separate the head from the neck. Then, cut the left ear, the forelock, the remaining ear pieces, and the remaining forelock pieces. Cut the right eye, then the back of the head, then the left eye. Proceed with the nostril, chin, and lower jaw. Make the blade entry holes for the vein and cut it. Finish with the neck, mane, and shoulder.

1 Outside edge
2 Separate head from neck
3 Left ear
4 Forelock
5 Remaining ear segments
6 Forelock
7 Right eye
8 Back of head
9 Left eye
10 Nostril, chin, lower jaw, vein
11 Neck, mane, shoulder

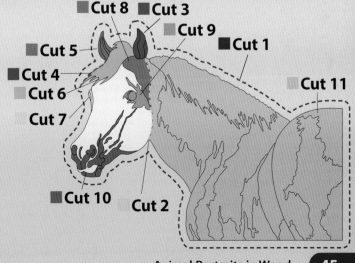

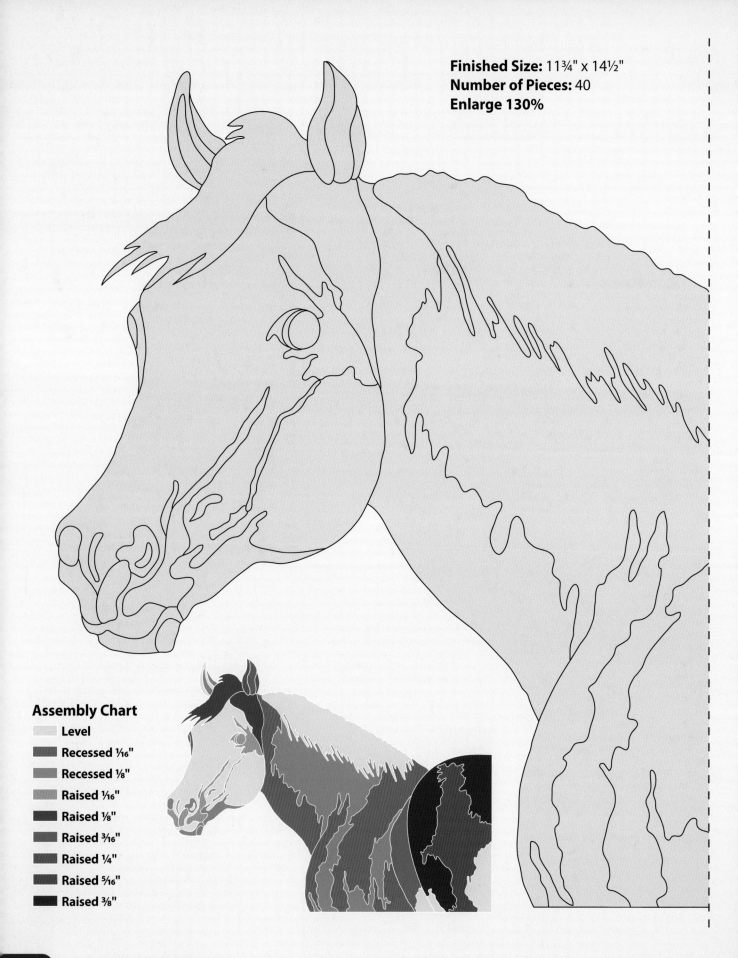

**Finished Size:** 11¾" x 14½"
**Number of Pieces:** 40
**Enlarge 130%**

**Assembly Chart**

Level
Recessed ¹⁄₁₆"
Recessed ⅛"
Raised ¹⁄₁₆"
Raised ⅛"
Raised ³⁄₁₆"
Raised ¼"
Raised ⁵⁄₁₆"
Raised ⅜"

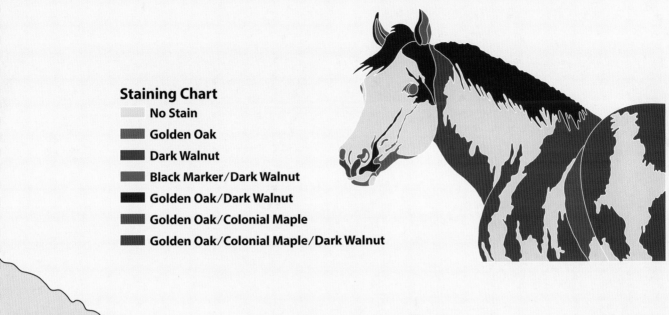

## Staining Chart

- No Stain
- Golden Oak
- Dark Walnut
- Black Marker/Dark Walnut
- Golden Oak/Dark Walnut
- Golden Oak/Colonial Maple
- Golden Oak/Colonial Maple/Dark Walnut

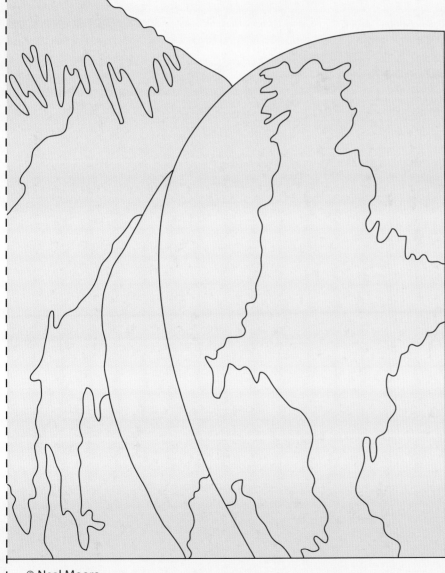

**Note:** The staining and assembly charts are meant only to provide a general guide for completing the projects. Remember to use the full-page photo of the finished project on page 44 and to modify the staining colors and assembly levels to suit your needs.

© Neal Moore

## CUTTING THE PATTERN

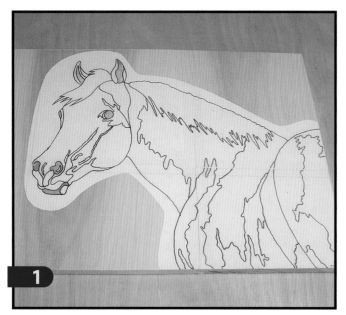

**1**

As in the previous projects, trim around the pattern leaving about a ½" margin. Attach the pattern to your wood of choice using temporary bond spray adhesive. Cut around the margin on the scroll saw to remove excess wood.

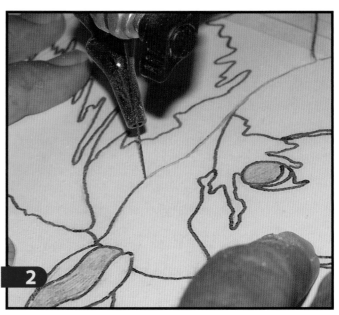

**2**

Starting on the pattern where the bottom of the jaw meets the bottom of the neck, cut on that line and exit the cut at the tip of the ear. The project has now been divided into two pieces. Place the larger piece aside and continue work on the head.

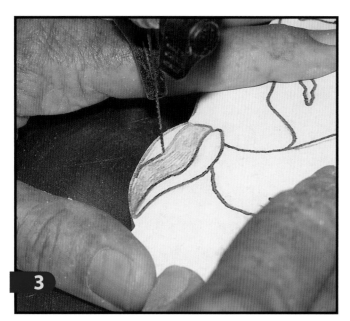

**3**

Cut out the segments for the mustang's left ear. Start, as shown, with the outer piece, and then remove the other two pieces in order.

**4**

Cut the line over the forelock of the mane to access the inside of the right ear. Remove that segment with one continuous cut.

**5**

Now, cut the remaining two segments of the ear. First, cut out the front piece, and then cut the back of the ear in that order.

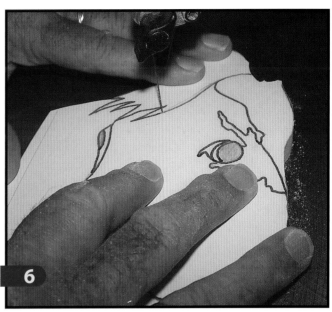

**6**

Cut out the forelock of the mane.

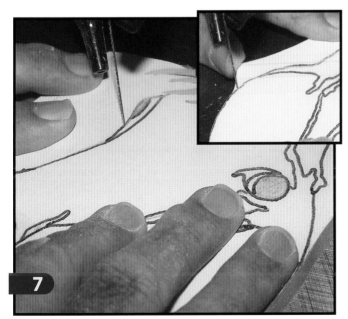

**7**

Start the next cut over the horse's right eye. Continue that cut down the bridge of the nose and around the tip of the nose, exiting at the point where you started the very first cut in the project.

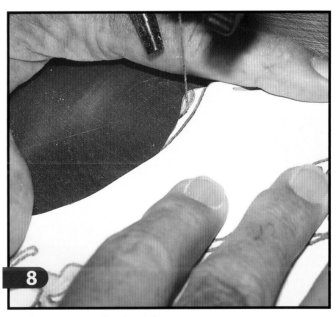

**8**

Cut the segments for the right eye.

## CUTTING THE PATTERN

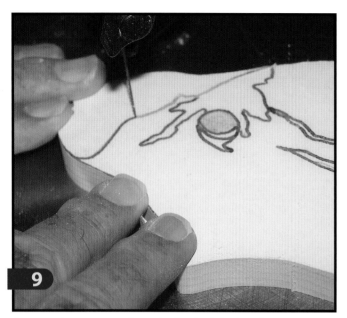

9

Remove the segment from the back of the head.

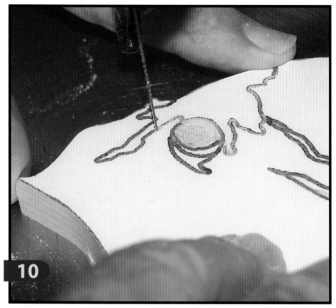

10

Cut the segment behind the horse's left eye. This will give you access to the eye segments so you don't need a blade entry hole.

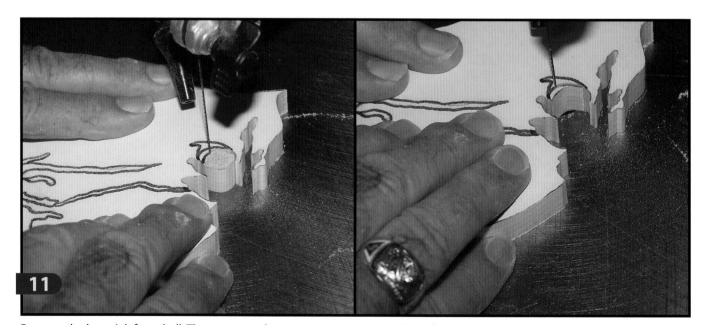

11

Remove the horse's left eyeball. Then, remove the next two eye segments in order.

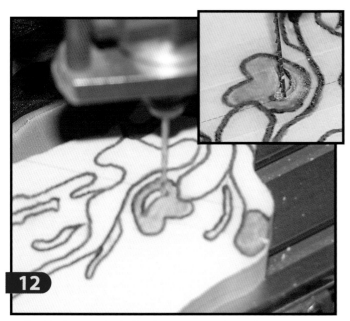

**12**

Drill a blade entry hole for the crescent-shaped segment in the left nostril and the small segment in the center of the nose. Then, thread the blade through the holes and remove those segments.

**13**

Remove the right nostril segment.

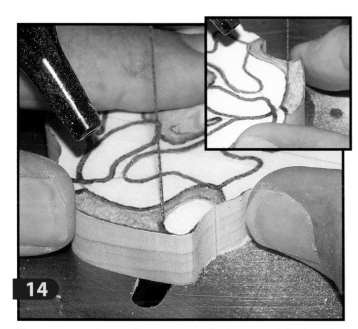

**14**

Then, remove the small segment at the bottom of the horse's chin. Remove the next segment in order.

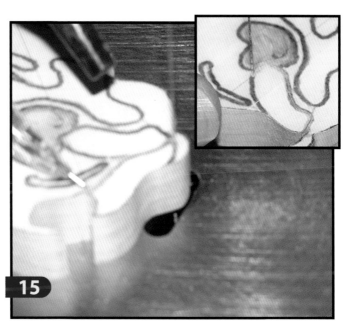

**15**

Start the next cut inside the horse's right nostril and cut that segment out. Remove the corresponding segments in order. Now you have access to the left nostril.

## CUTTING THE PATTERN

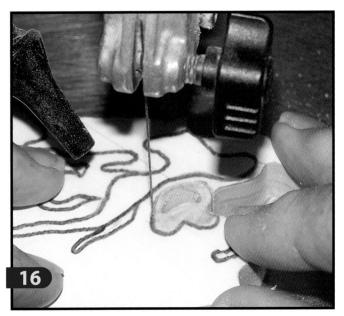

**16**

Remove the left nostril.

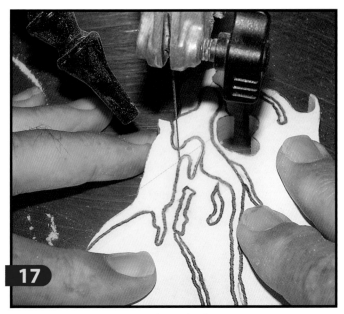

**17**

Then, remove the segment from the lower jaw.

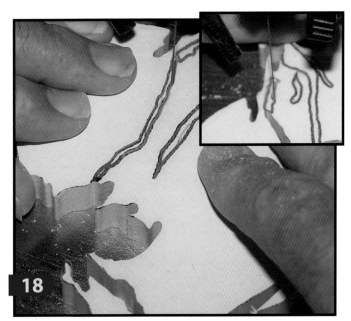

**18**

Starting the next cut under the horse's left eye, remove the long, thin segment that represents the vein running down the jaw. Next, remove the small segment below that in order.

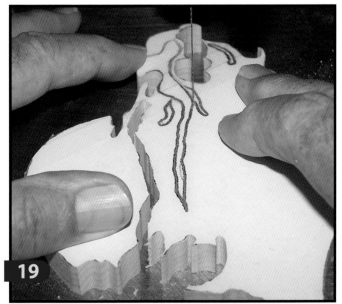

**19**

Start your next cut where you see my left index finger in the photo. Remove that segment with one continuous cut. This will provide access to the smaller segments on each side.

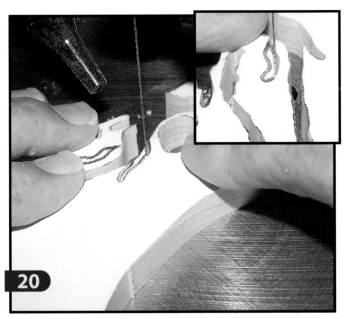

**20**

Remove the small segment, as shown, and then remove the remaining small segment (see inset photo). This should complete all of the cuts for the horse's head.

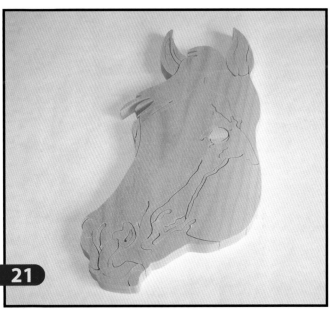

**21**

Remove the pattern paper from the segments, and assemble the horse's head near your staining materials.

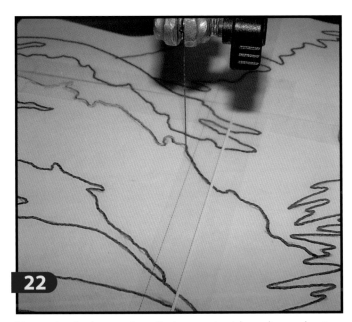

**22**

Now, take the larger piece that you set aside earlier and cut on the pattern line, following the line around the back of the mane and exiting the pattern.

**23**

Continue cutting the segments from the neck, mane, and shoulders and assemble those segments with the head.

## CUTTING THE PATTERN

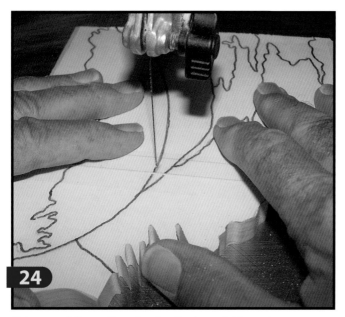

**24**

Cut around the pattern line for the horse's hip and exit the pattern.

**25**

Cut all of the remaining segments and assemble them to the rest of the horse in preparation for staining. Ensure no sawdust remains on the segments.

## STAINING THE PIECES

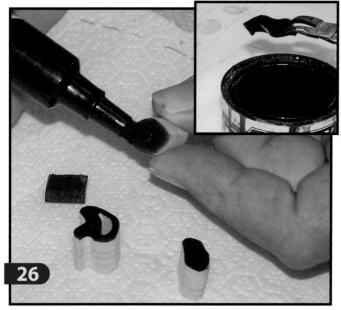

**26**

Color the segments for the eyes, nostrils, and bottom of the mouth with the black permanent marker. Dip each piece in dark walnut stain and place them aside, face up, to dry. Use the staining chart on page 47 and the full-page photo on page 44 to aid you as you stain the project.

**27**

Dip the two segments that were cut in Step 15 in dark walnut stain. Wipe off some of the stain with an old rag so the segments are not too dark.

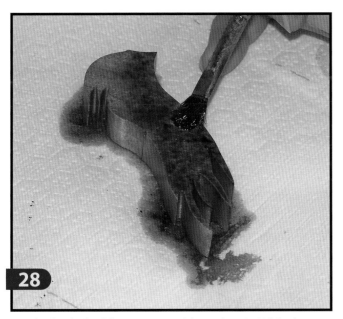

**28**

Dip the forelock of the mane in golden oak stain. While the stain is still wet, smear mix dark walnut stain in the golden oak.

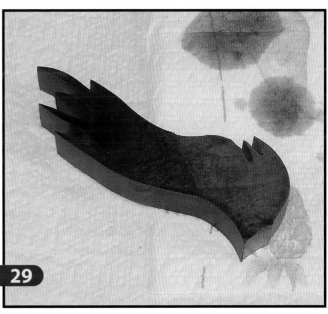

**29**

The stain will blend from dark to light from the bottom of the segment to the top.

**30**

Dip the segment that was cut in Step 17 in golden oak stain and place it aside to dry.

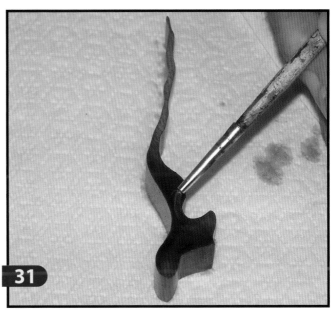

**31**

Now dip the segment that was cut in Step 19 in golden oak stain. While the stain is still wet, smear mix dark walnut on the larger end of the segment and blend dark to light, bottom to top.

## STAINING THE PIECES

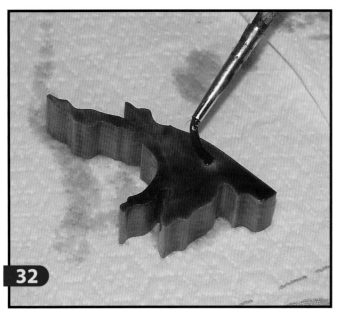

**32**

Stain the segment that was cut from behind the left eye with golden oak. Smear mix dark walnut to create a darker edge where this segment joins the neck.

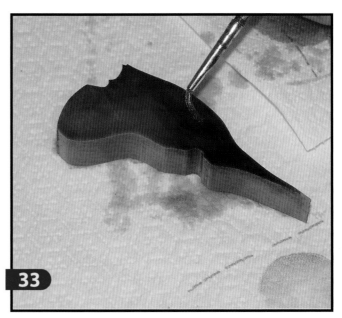

**33**

Stain the segment that forms the back of the head golden oak, and then smear mix dark walnut, as shown.

**34**

The remaining segments from the horse's face pieces, which represent veins in the horse's face, are stained golden oak and placed aside to dry.

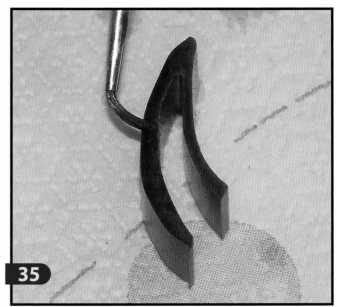

**35**

Dip the front of the ear in golden oak and smear mix dark walnut into it to create an uneven shade of brown.

**36**

Stain the mane golden oak and smear mix dark walnut into it to create a dark mane with some lighter highlights.

**37**

Stain the segment that forms the lower neck golden oak. Then, while it is still wet, use a brush and flood the surface with colonial maple. In this step, you want to achieve an even, reddish-orange color.

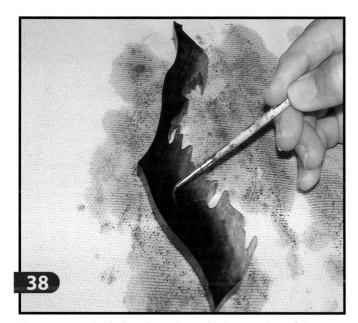

**38**

Now, smear mix dark walnut along the lower edge of the segment, as shown. The goal is a dark-to-light transition across the segment with no hard edge.

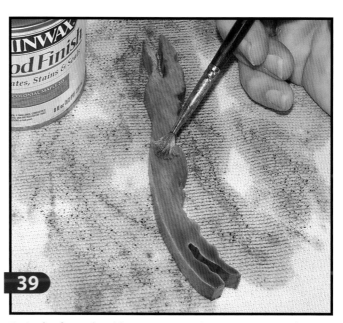

**39**

Stain the front shoulder segment in the same manner: first with golden oak, then flood with colonial maple.

## Staining the Pieces

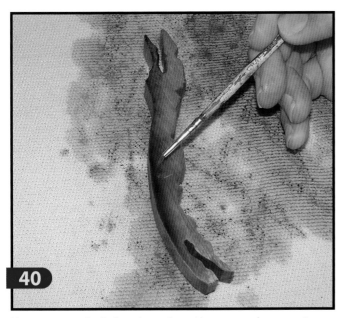

**40**

Next, smear mix dark walnut along the outer edge, creating a gradual dark to light blend.

**41**

Stain the next segment for the horse's side. Again, use golden oak and flood with colonial maple.

**42**

Then, smear mix dark walnut from the top down, as shown.

**43**

Stain the segment for the horse's belly golden oak, flooded with colonial maple. No dark walnut is applied to this segment.

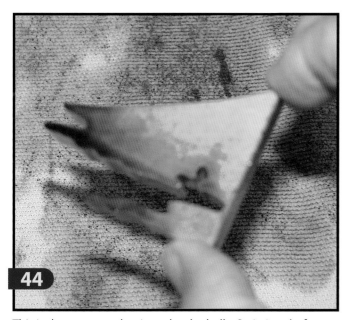

44

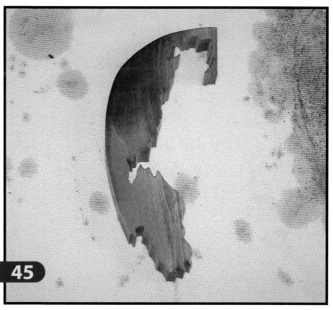

45

This is the segment that is under the belly. Stain it as before, with golden oak and then colonial maple, and smear mix dark walnut. While wet, this segment can be tipped from side to side, as shown in the photo, to let the dark walnut stain form a smooth transition from dark to light.

Stain the remaining segment golden oak, flooded with colonial maple, and smear mix dark walnut on the upper part of the horse's hip. All remaining pieces stay unstained. Once all of the pieces are dry, the project is ready to be assembled.

## ASSEMBLING THE PROJECT

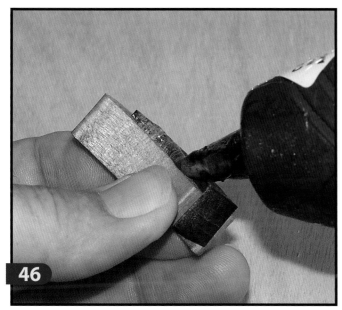

46

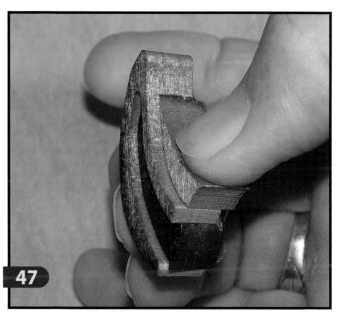

47

Recess the inside of the horse's right ear, with respect to the outer part of the ear, about ⅛". While holding it in position, glue the pieces together on the back side. As you go through the assembly process, remember to refer to the assembly chart on page 47 for additional information.

Now, recess the small segment that represents the back of the right ear about ⅛" with respect to the front of the ear. Glue the pieces from the back side. Place this assembled ear aside until later.

## ASSEMBLING THE PROJECT

**48**

Hold the three segments for the left ear in position so the dark center segment is recessed about ⅛" with respect to the front of the other two segments. Make sure the three pieces fit snugly together and glue them up from the back. Place this ear aside with the right ear.

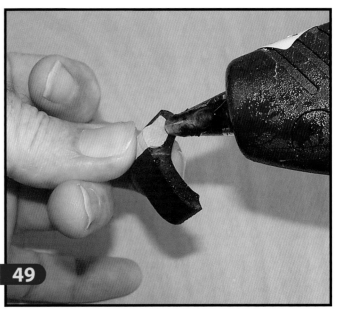

**49**

Position the small light segment in place in the black chin segment. Hold the pieces so the surfaces are flush with each other and glue them together.

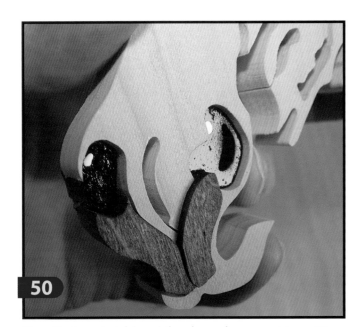

**50**

Place the horse's right nostril and muzzle segment in position. Recess the nostril and elevate the muzzle segment about ⅛". Position the other nostril and muzzle segment in the same manner and glue them up from the back.

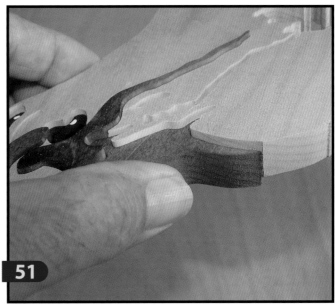

**51**

Elevate about 1/16" the long, thin segment that runs back the horse's face, recess the segment under the jaw about ⅛", and glue these segments together. Glue the remaining small segments in the horse's face, elevating each about 1/16".

**52**

Position the four segments for the eye, as shown, and glue them in. The surfaces of all four segments should be flush with each other and elevated about 1/16".

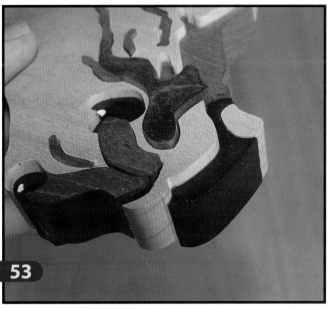

**53**

Position the horse's mouth and chin, as shown, and glue them in.

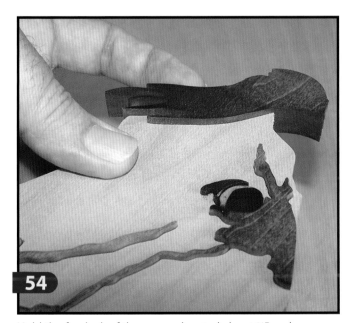

**54**

Hold the forelock of the mane elevated about 1/8" and glue it in place.

**55**

Glue the two segments for the right eye in place. I used wood glue for this step because there is very little surface on the back of these small pieces for hot glue.

## ASSEMBLING THE PROJECT

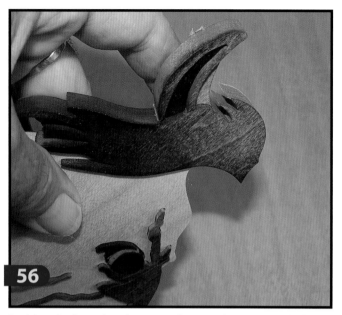

**56**

Position the horse's right ear in place on the mane and glue it on. The ear should be recessed about ⅛".

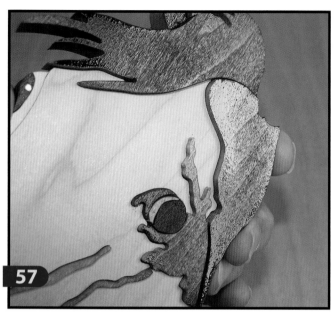

**57**

Glue the last segment for the head at the same elevation as the forelock of the mane.

**58**

Position the mane in place so it is elevated about ⅛" and glue it on.

**59**

Next, position the bottom of the neck so it is elevated about ¹⁄₁₆" and glue it on.

60

Hold the next two segments in place, elevated ¹⁄₁₆", and glue them on.

61

Next, glue the corresponding light segment in place at the same elevation as the other light segment.

62

Glue the next dark segment on at the same elevation as the previous dark segments.

63

Position the belly segment. Elevate this segment ¼" higher than the previous segment and glue it on.

## ASSEMBLING THE PROJECT

64

Position the flank, or hip segment, ¼" higher than the belly segment and glue it on.

65

Glue the remaining large, light segment so it is recessed ¹⁄₁₆" lower than the hip segment. Glue in the last two small, light segments at the same elevation as the previous segment.

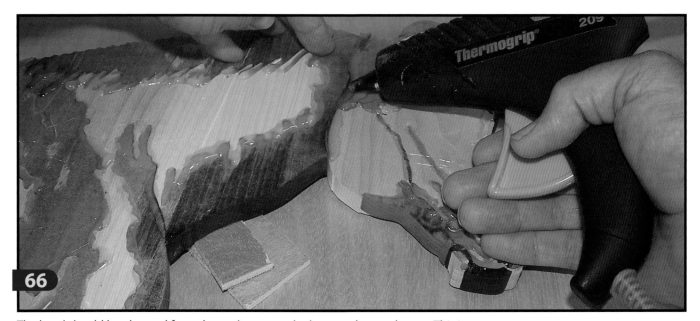

66

The head should be elevated from the neck more at the bottom than at the top. This is done with a shim. A shim is basically an additional board, temporarily placed between the project and the work table, that lends extra height to a certain part of the finished project. Place the whole project face down on the layout board. Place the shim under the bottom of the neck so it is raised ¼". Position the head face down and flat on the layout board. While holding the top of the neck flush with the top of the head, glue the two pieces together. Continue holding the top until the glue sets; then, remove the shim.

67

Position the left ear so it is elevated ⅛" and glue it on.

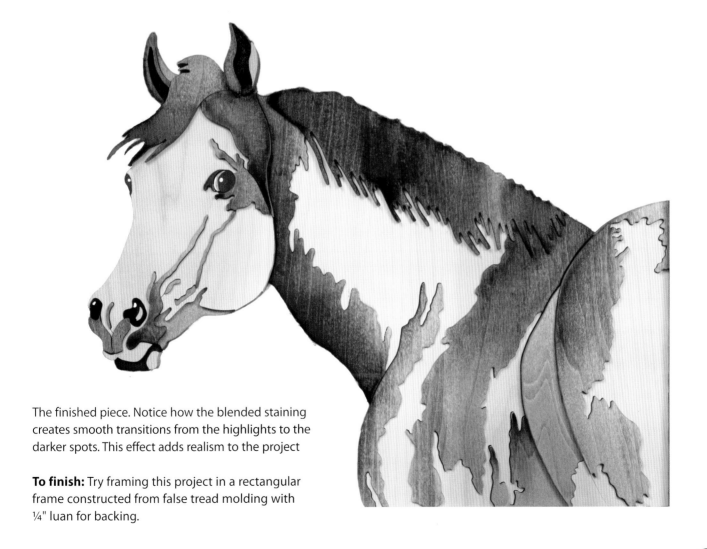

The finished piece. Notice how the blended staining creates smooth transitions from the highlights to the darker spots. This effect adds realism to the project

**To finish:** Try framing this project in a rectangular frame constructed from false tread molding with ¼" luan for backing.

# PART FOUR

# PROJECTS

I chose the projects in this section because they are some of my favorite species of wildlife and because they lend themselves well to segmented portraiture. *The Great Horned Owl* was chosen to open this section because it is a natural progression from the three demonstration projects.

Although the following projects have some segments that are more complex and will be more of a challenge to cut than those in the demonstrations, the steps for cutting, staining, and assembling the pieces are generally the same. Because you have learned the basic skills from the three demonstrations in Part Three, less instruction is included for each of the projects in this section. For each portrait, however, I have highlighted some of the important areas specific to that piece.

The skills you learned in the demonstration section will be employed in the projects, and new skills, especially cutting, will be developed. Each

remaining portrait will increase in complexity, and the skills developed in each previous project will be applied to the next.

Any and all of the patterns provided here may be altered as you see fit. I encourage you to develop your own style and, if you choose, change pattern lines and shading or incorporate more or less relief to make these portraits your own creations. I have simply provided patterns and recommendations to get your creative juices flowing.

As you progress through the projects, I hope that you discover the best methods for your working style and that they result in a truly personalized portrait. If so, I know you will enjoy this wonderful art form, and this book will have achieved its intended purpose.

# THE GREAT HORNED OWL

"Great horned owl" is the common name for the only American representative of a group of large owls called eagle owls. This owl derives its name from its conspicuous ear tufts, or "horns." Great horned owls occupy a great variety of habitats, from subarctic coniferous forests to arid deserts and wooded city parks. They will feed on almost any living prey that they can overpower, such as mice, birds, reptiles, fish, and even small dogs. They are among the few predators of skunks, whose scent often permeates the owls' plumage. Great horned owls are my favorite owls, probably as a result of often hearing their eerie calls in the predawn hours while sitting in a deer stand.

To begin, enlarge this pattern to at least 115% to facilitate cutting the tiny, fragile tips that appear in the owl's face. A #2 blade should be used for all of these intricate cuts.

## Tools and Materials

- ◆ Light-colored, soft wood of choice (poplar), ½" to ¾" thick, sized to fit the pattern
- ◆ Scroll saw
- ◆ #5 reverse skip-tooth blades for general cuts
- ◆ #2 reverse skip-tooth blades for intricate cuts
- ◆ Temporary bond spray adhesive
- ◆ Drill or drill press
- ◆ ¹⁄₁₆" drill bit
- ◆ Sandpaper, small square of 120 grit
- ◆ Wax paper or butcher paper, large sheet
- ◆ Paper towels, one roll, or rags
- ◆ Small tongs or pliers
- ◆ Golden oak stain, one 32 oz. can
- ◆ Dark walnut stain, one 32 oz. can
- ◆ Colonial maple stain, one 32 oz. can
- ◆ Brushes, small and medium
- ◆ Black permanent marker
- ◆ Aluminum baking pans
- ◆ White acrylic paint or gesso
- ◆ Hot glue gun
- ◆ Glue sticks
- ◆ Wood glue, small bottle

## TIPS FOR COMPLETING THE PROJECT

- ◆ Divide the project into two pieces by separating the owl's face from its neck.
- ◆ Cut away the ears and the cheek ruff to expose the eye; then, move from left to right across the face, cutting the eye segments first.
- ◆ Drill blade entry holes for the variegated area on the owl's neck. Make these pierced cuts while you still have sufficient stock to hold on to.
- ◆ Create a yellow tone for the eyes and ears by wiping off golden oak stain before it has a chance to soak into the wood.
- ◆ Smear dark walnut stain onto golden oak to achieve a mottled appearance on the forehead, ears, and body.
- ◆ Position the head on the body and push it up or down until you are satisfied with the relief between the head and the body.
- ◆ Display the owl in a 13" x 16" poplar frame made from false tread molding and stained golden oak. The ¼" luan backing was stained colonial maple.

Separate the face and neck.

Cut the ears and cheek to expose the eye.

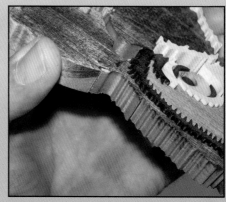
Notice the depth of the owl's eye.

**Finished Size:** 8⅜" x 11½"
**Number of Pieces:** 41
**Enlarge 115%**

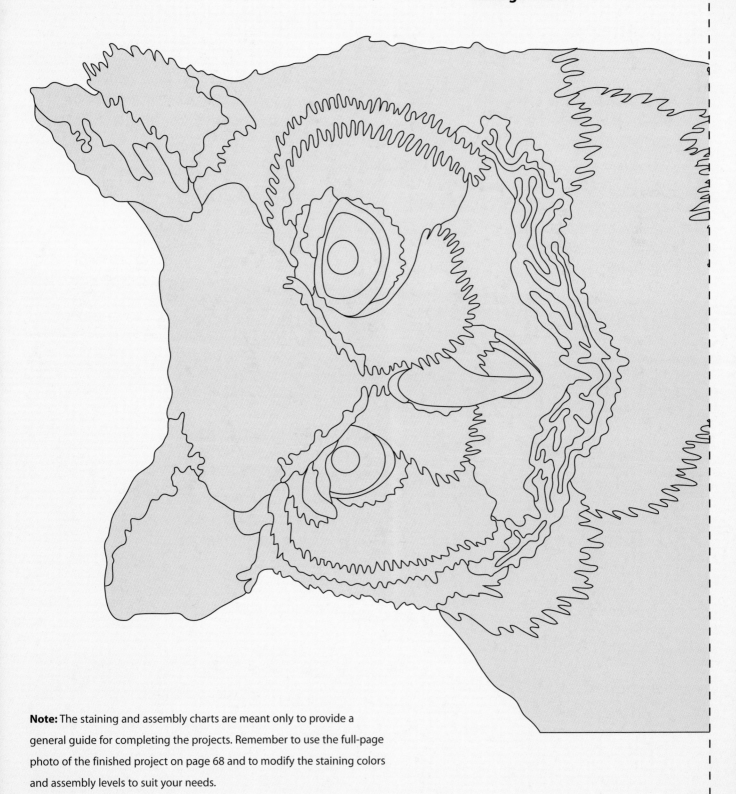

**Note:** The staining and assembly charts are meant only to provide a general guide for completing the projects. Remember to use the full-page photo of the finished project on page 68 and to modify the staining colors and assembly levels to suit your needs.

**Staining Chart**

No Stain

Golden Oak

Colonial Maple

Dark Walnut

Black Marker/Dark Walnut

Golden Oak/Dark Walnut

**Assembly Chart**

Level

Recessed ⅛"

Raised ⅟₁₆"

Raised ⅛"

Raised ³⁄₁₆"

Raised ¼"

Raised ⁵⁄₁₆"

Raised ⅜"

Raised ⁷⁄₁₆"

Raised ½"

Raised ⁹⁄₁₆"

Raised ⅝"

© Neal Moore

# THE WHITE-TAILED BUCK

One of the most popular big game animals among American hunters, the whitetail has made an amazing comeback in the past 50 years. This once scarce deer is now a common sight in most, if not all, of the eastern United States.

This animal has provided me with countless hours of outdoor enjoyment, and even though I no longer hunt deer for sport, I would be remiss in not including him here. To begin, enlarge the pattern to 130%. You can make it larger if desired, even up to life size.

## Tools and Materials

- ◆ **Light-colored, soft wood of choice (poplar), ½" to ¾" thick, sized to fit the pattern**
- ◆ **Scroll saw**
- ◆ **#5 reverse skip-tooth blades for general cuts**
- ◆ **#2 reverse skip-tooth blades for intricate cuts**
- ◆ **Temporary bond spray adhesive**
- ◆ **Drill or drill press**
- ◆ **1⁄16" drill bit**
- ◆ **Sandpaper, small square of 120 grit**
- ◆ **Wax paper or butcher paper, large sheet**
- ◆ **Paper towels, one roll, or rags**
- ◆ **Small tongs or pliers**
- ◆ **Golden oak stain, one 32 oz. can**
- ◆ **Dark walnut stain, one 32 oz. can**
- ◆ **Brushes, small and medium**
- ◆ **Black permanent marker**
- ◆ **Aluminum baking pans**
- ◆ **White acrylic paint or gesso**
- ◆ **Hot glue gun**
- ◆ **Glue sticks**
- ◆ **Wood glue, small bottle**

## TIPS FOR COMPLETING THE PROJECT

- ◆ Cut the project into three pieces to make it easier to handle on the saw table. First, remove both antlers, and then separate the two antlers.
- ◆ You will need wood glue in two places on this project: to glue the small antler tips to the antlers and to glue the antlers to the head (to alleviate the stress the glue joint might encounter due to the weight of the antlers).
- ◆ Mount on a natural slab oval, frame, or display as is.

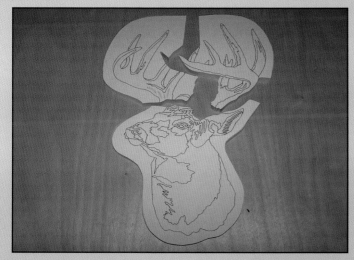

First, remove both antlers.

Wood glue helps strengthen the antlers.

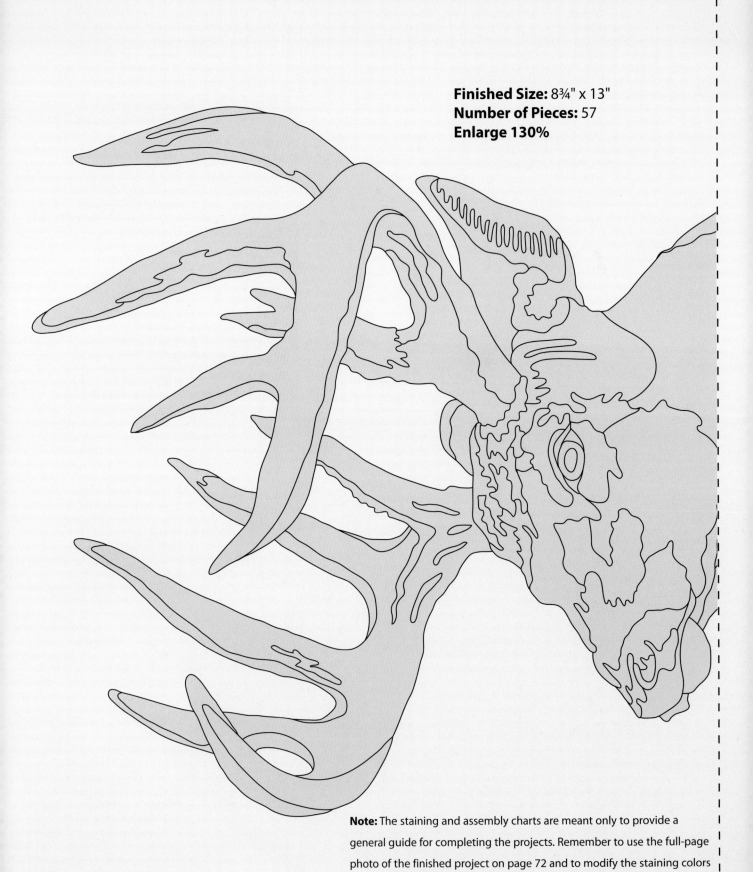

**Finished Size:** 8¾" x 13"
**Number of Pieces:** 57
**Enlarge 130%**

**Note:** The staining and assembly charts are meant only to provide a general guide for completing the projects. Remember to use the full-page photo of the finished project on page 72 and to modify the staining colors and assembly levels to suit your needs.

## Staining Chart

- No Stain
- Golden Oak
- Dark Walnut
- Black Marker/Dark Walnut
- Golden Oak/Dark Walnut

## Assembly Chart

- Level
- Recessed 1/16"
- Recessed 1/8"
- Raised 1/16"
- Raised 1/8"
- Raised 3/16"
- Raised 1/4"
- Raised 5/16"
- Raised 3/8"

© Neal Moore

# THE GIRAFFE

The giraffe is the tallest living animal and is instantly recognized by its exceptionally long neck. Male giraffes average about 17 feet tall, but some grow to a height of almost 20 feet.

I really like this pattern because it captures a graceful and serene profile that seems so uncharacteristic of an animal perceived as ungainly and awkward. I find beauty in all of God's creatures, and I suppose this, and all the other projects, is my way of having a trophy to hang on the wall and still preserve the life of the species depicted. To begin, enlarge this pattern at least 160% to facilitate pierce cutting the small spots on the giraffe's face.

## Tools and Materials

- ◆ **Light-colored, soft wood of choice (poplar),** ½" to ¾" thick, sized to fit the pattern
- ◆ **Scroll saw**
- ◆ **#5 reverse skip-tooth blades for general cuts**
- ◆ **#2 reverse skip-tooth blades for intricate cuts**
- ◆ **Temporary bond spray adhesive**
- ◆ **Drill or drill press**
- ◆ **¹⁄₁₆" drill bit**
- ◆ **Sandpaper, small square of 120 grit**
- ◆ **Wax paper or butcher paper, large sheet**
- ◆ **Paper towels, one roll, or rags**
- ◆ **Small tongs or pliers**
- ◆ **2 pieces ¼" x 24" x 24" luan plywood,** or stiff cardboard
- ◆ **Golden oak stain, one 32 oz. can**
- ◆ **Dark walnut stain, one 32 oz. can**
- ◆ **Colonial maple stain, one 32 oz. can**
- ◆ **Brushes, small and medium**
- ◆ **Black permanent marker**
- ◆ **Aluminum baking pans**
- ◆ **White acrylic paint or gesso**
- ◆ **Hot glue gun**
- ◆ **Glue sticks**
- ◆ **Wood glue, small bottle**

## TIPS FOR COMPLETING THE PROJECT

- ◆ Edge glue and clamp two or more ½"-thick boards of sufficient width and length to accommodate the pattern.
- ◆ Use a #2 blade for the smaller spots and the eye; use the #5 for the remaining segments.
- ◆ Cut the pattern into three smaller pieces: neck, antlers and forehead, and face.
- ◆ Once the project has been cut into manageable pieces, drill blade entry holes for any spots that cannot be removed using continuous cuts.
- ◆ Divide the giraffe into a head section and a neck section, and glue them separately to make it easier to handle.
- ◆ Dark walnut smear mixed around the edges of the spots and dragged into golden oak will create a highlight in the center of the darker edges.
- ◆ Use colonial maple stain and a small artist's brush to add the reddish-orange highlights to the segments, as seen in the photo on page 76. Dip the brush in the stain, and then wipe the brush on a paper towel to remove most of the stain. Then, "dry brush" the highlights on the segment.
- ◆ Display this piece mounted in a rectangular frame.

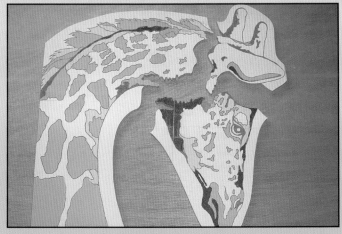

Cut the pattern into three smaller pieces.

Smear mix dark walnut around spots' edges.

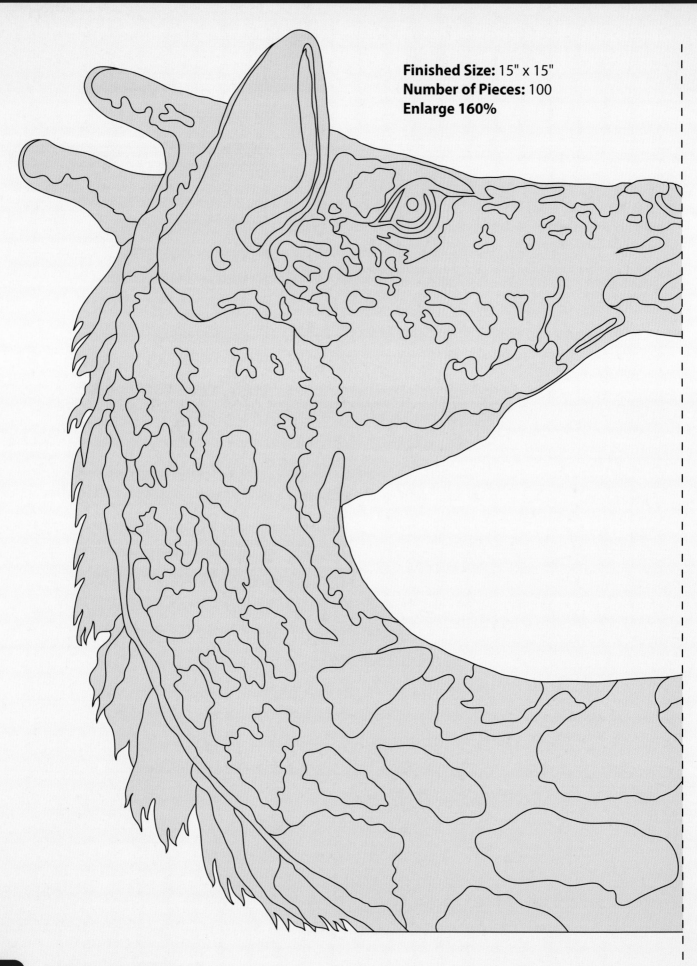

**Finished Size:** 15" x 15"
**Number of Pieces:** 100
**Enlarge 160%**

**Note:** The staining and assembly charts are meant only to provide a general guide for completing the projects. Remember to use the full-page photo of the finished project on page 76 and to modify the staining colors and assembly levels to suit your needs.

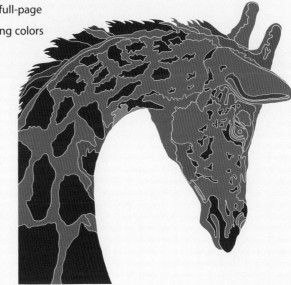

## Staining Chart

| | |
|---|---|
| | No Stain |
| | Golden Oak |
| | Dark Walnut |
| | Black Marker/Dark Walnut |
| | Golden Oak/Dark Walnut |
| | Golden Oak/Colonial Maple |

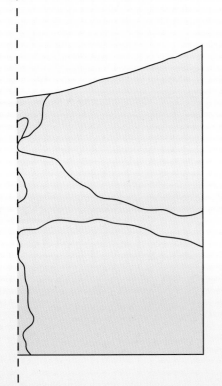

## Assembly Chart

| | |
|---|---|
| | Level |
| | Recessed ¹⁄₁₆" |
| | Recessed ⅛" |
| | Raised ¹⁄₁₆" |
| | Raised ⅛" |
| | Raised ³⁄₁₆" |
| | Raised ¼" |
| | Raised ⁵⁄₁₆" |
| | Raised ⅜" |

© Neal Moore

# THE WOLF

There are two species of wolves. The gray, or timber, wolf was once widely distributed but is now only found in Canada, Alaska, and northern Europe and Russia. The red wolf, virtually extinct in the wild, is now found only in Texas and the southeastern United States.

This project is a timber wolf portrait. I chose to include him because, to me, he represents everything we love about wildlife and the wilderness. He is a survivor. To capture his majesty, enlarge the pattern at least 105%.

## Tools and Materials

- Light-colored, soft wood of choice (poplar), ½" to ¾" thick, sized to fit the pattern
- Scroll saw
- #5 reverse skip-tooth blades for general cuts
- #2 reverse skip-tooth blades for intricate cuts
- Temporary bond spray adhesive
- Drill or drill press
- ⅟₁₆" drill bit
- Sandpaper, small square of 120 grit
- Wax paper or butcher paper, large sheet
- Paper towels, one roll, or rags
- Small tongs or pliers
- Golden oak stain, one 32 oz. can
- Dark walnut stain, one 32 oz. can
- Brushes, small and medium
- Black permanent marker
- Aluminum baking pans
- White acrylic paint or gesso
- Hot glue gun
- Glue sticks
- Wood glue, small bottle

## TIPS FOR COMPLETING THE PROJECT

- Start the cuts at the ears with a #2 blade. Cut with care to keep the fragile tips where hair is simulated intact.
- After cutting several segments, start reassembling the image to prevent fragile tips from being accidentally broken off.
- Stain all of the black pieces first. Color those surfaces with a black permanent marker to achieve a very dark black; then, stain them with dark walnut.
- Most of this project is stained golden oak, then smear mixed with dark walnut for highlights.
- Set the ears back slightly on the head. Recess the eyes similar to those of a real wolf.
- The nose and the center of the bridge of the nose are the highest reference points.
- Frame on a light background; the edge detail gets lost on a darker background.

Cut and assemble carefully to keep fragile tips intact.

Recess the ears from the head.

**Finished Size:** 7" x 10"
**Number of Pieces:** 55
**Enlarge 105%**

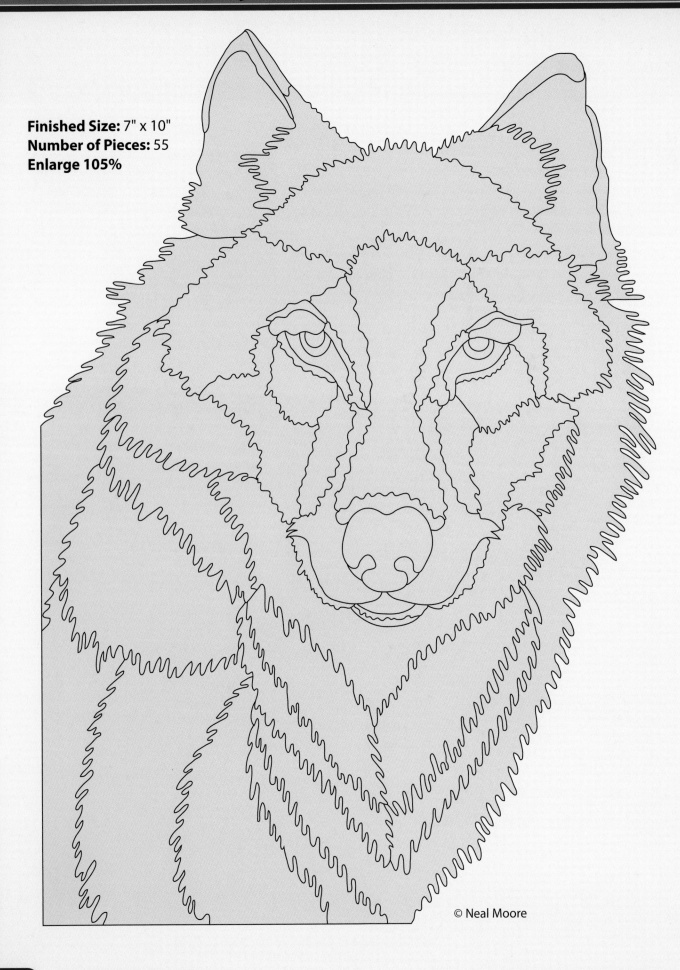

© Neal Moore

## Staining Chart

▨ **No Stain**

▨ **Golden Oak**

▨ **Dark Walnut**

▨ **Black Marker/Dark Walnut**

▨ **Golden Oak/Dark Walnut**

**Note:** The staining and assembly charts are meant only to provide a general guide for completing the projects. Remember to use the full-page photo of the finished project on page 80 and to modify the staining colors and assembly levels to suit your needs.

## Assembly Chart

▨ **Level**

▨ **Recessed 1/16"**

▨ **Recessed 1/8"**

▨ **Raised 1/16"**

▨ **Raised 1/8"**

▨ **Raised 3/16"**

▨ **Raised 1/4"**

▨ **Raised 5/16"**

▨ **Raised 3/8"**

# THE BARN OWL

Barn owls differ from typical owls in that they have a heart-shaped face, longer legs, and smaller eyes. Additionally, their eyes are never yellow as are most owls'.

I have seen many of these birds in the wild, mostly in abandoned barns where they nest or silently gliding over a freshly mowed hayfield in the evening in search of mice. To begin, enlarge the pattern to 120%.

## TIPS FOR COMPLETING THE PROJECT

- Work in this order to neatly remove the small wing feathers: 1) cut the complete wing from the owl, 2) remove the upper part of the wing from the lower, 3) cut each of the small feathers from the first row. This approach allows you to start the blade at 90 degrees to the work and make a clean exit.

- Reassemble the small feathers as you cut them out because they are easy to mix up. Correct spacing of the small row of feathers can be a problem. I held the piece upside down and placed each feather in position and glued them individually. I did the second row the same way.

- Reassemble the project starting with the head; then, glue the large part of the wing and the back to the body.

- The large primary feathers were glued flush with each other, but you can add relief to them as well if you wish.

- Glue the feet so that the two toes on the near leg are elevated higher than the two toes visible on the far leg.

- Create spots by lightly touching a small brush loaded with dark walnut stain to the segment. These spots tend to spread out rapidly, so don't load the brush too heavily. The stain should form a round spot, which will be lighter in the center with a darker ring around the circumference when it dries. After it dries, go back and paint a small white dot of white acrylic paint or gesso in the center of each spot.

- Display the owl as is with a sawtooth hanger so it hangs straight on the wall or frame it with a luan backing.

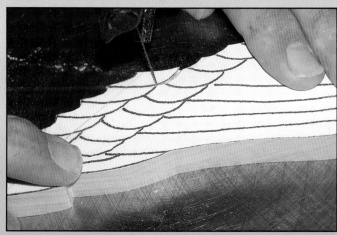

Cut each of the small feathers in the first row.

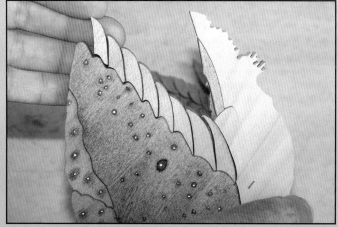

Create spots with dark walnut stain.

**Finished Size:** 10" x 12"
**Number of Pieces:** 56
**Enlarge 120%**

**Note:** The staining and assembly charts are meant only to provide a general guide for completing the projects. Remember to use the full-page photo of the finished project on page 84 and to modify the staining colors and assembly levels to suit your needs.

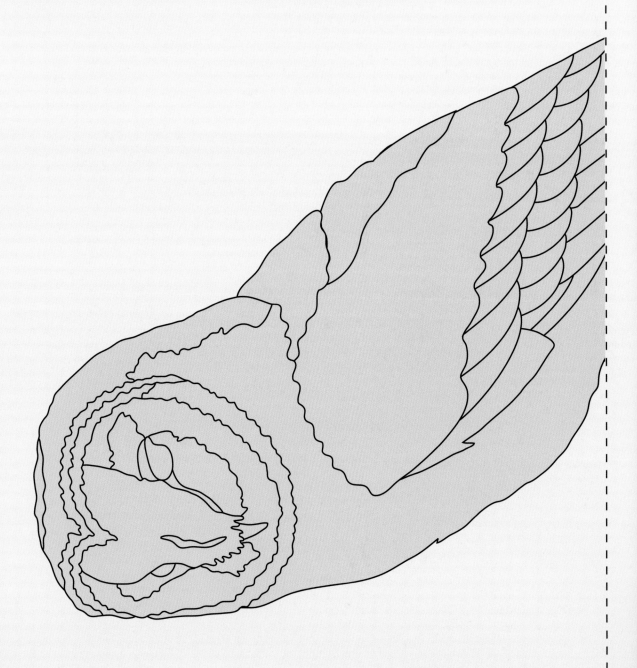

**Staining Chart**

No Stain
Golden Oak
Colonial Maple
Dark Walnut
Black Marker/Dark Walnut
Golden Oak/Dark Walnut

**Assembly Chart**

Level
Recessed ¹⁄₁₆"
Recessed ⅛"
Raised ¹⁄₁₆"
Raised ⅛"
Raised ³⁄₁₆"
Raised ¼"
Raised ⁵⁄₁₆"
Raised ⅜"

© Neal Moore

# THE JAGUAR

The jaguar is the largest and most powerful of the American members of the cat family. He is found from the southern United States to northern Argentina but is especially abundant in the dense forests of Central America and Brazil. He is a great climber, and the image in this project gives the impression that he is stalking prey that has caught his deadly attention.

Although I am fascinated by the power and beauty of all of the great predatory cats, I think the jaguar's coat is the most beautiful. There are about 180 pieces in this project, consisting mostly of spots. To begin, enlarge the pattern about 130% or smaller, as long as the smaller spots are large enough to cut.

## TIPS FOR COMPLETING THE PROJECT

- Edge glue two or more boards of ½" stock to accommodate the pattern.
- Separate the face from the rest of the jaguar's body.
- Drill the blade entry holes for the spots just inside and touching the pattern lines so the holes will be concealed by the dark stain.
- Cut all of the spots first; then, cut segments from the outside in. Plan your cuts so that you cut larger segments and then remove smaller segments from them.
- Assemble the pieces as you go until the complete pattern has been cut out.
- Five pieces are very light, but not white: the two crescent-shaped parts of the eyes, the two segments on each side of the bridge of the nose, and the piece just inside the cat's left ear. Dip each of these pieces in golden oak, and then wipe most of the stain off with a soft, lint-free rag.
- Stain the eyeballs with golden oak, and, while they're still wet, place a tiny drop of dark walnut in the center of each eyeball.
- The nose is the highest point, and the eyes are the lowest.
- Frame the jaguar with a luan backing; he does not work well as a stand-alone portrait.

### Tools and Materials

- Light-colored, soft wood of choice (poplar), ½" to ¾" thick, sized to fit the pattern
- Scroll saw
- #5 reverse skip-tooth blades for general cuts
- #2 reverse skip-tooth blades for intricate cuts
- Temporary bond spray adhesive
- Drill or drill press
- ⅟₁₆" drill bit
- Sandpaper, small square of 120 grit
- Wax paper or butcher paper, large sheet
- Paper towels, one roll, or rags
- Soft, lint-free rag
- Small tongs or pliers
- 2 pieces ¼" x 24" x 24" luan plywood, or stiff cardboard
- Golden oak stain, one 32 oz. can
- Dark walnut stain, one 32 oz. can
- Colonial maple stain, one 32 oz. can
- Brushes, small and medium
- Black permanent marker
- Aluminum baking pans
- White acrylic paint or gesso
- Hot glue gun
- Glue sticks
- Wood glue, small bottle

Work from the back to glue the spots.

The eyes are the lowest point of the project.

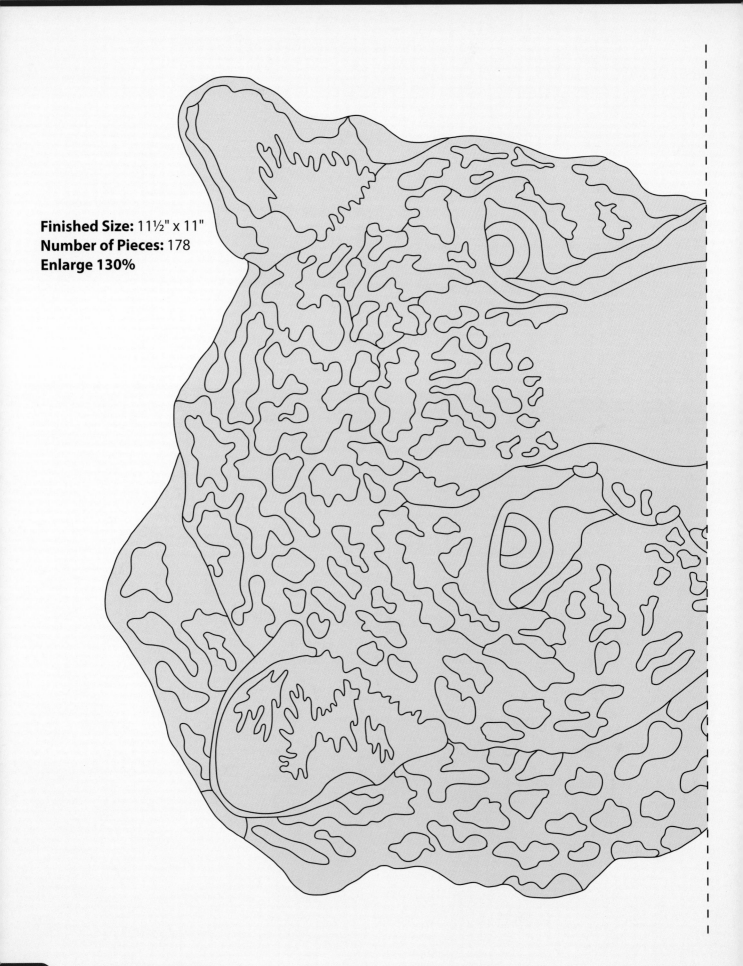

**Finished Size:** 11½" x 11"
**Number of Pieces:** 178
**Enlarge 130%**

**Note:** The staining and assembly charts are meant only to provide a general guide for completing the projects. Remember to use the full-page photo of the finished project on page 88 and to modify the staining colors and assembly levels to suit your needs.

## Staining Chart

No Stain
Golden Oak
Colonial Maple
Dark Walnut
Black Marker / Dark Walnut
Golden Oak / Dark Walnut
Colonial Maple / Dark Walnut

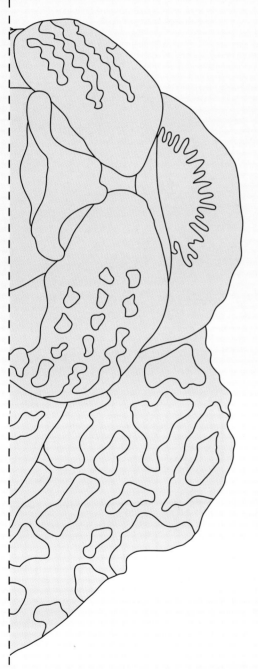

## Assembly Chart

Level
Raised ⅛"
Raised 3/16"
Raised ¼"
Raised 5/16"
Raised ⅜"
Raised 7/16"
Raised ½"
Raised 9/16"
Raised ⅝"
Raised 11/16"

© Neal Moore

# THE BOBCAT

Although this fellow is widespread throughout the United States, he is seldom seen in the wild. His close relative, the Canadian lynx, is considered endangered and is protected in the lower 48 states.

I have been fortunate enough to see one of these cats in the wild in my home state of West Virginia but was only able to observe him for about thirty seconds before he quietly disappeared into the underbrush. I chose him for a subject because, pound for pound, he is as impressive as any of his larger cousins. To begin, enlarge the pattern to 125%.

## TIPS FOR COMPLETING THE PROJECT

- Exercise caution when cutting. This pattern includes hundreds of tiny, fragile tips that represent hair, and they will not tolerate much pressure from your fingers as you guide the wood into the saw blade. Change the blade at the first signs of dulling.
- Remove the ears first; then, separate the head into two pieces.
- Use a #2 blade to cut the spots, removing all of the spots first.
- Take special care when cutting around the eyes to maintain the integrity of the pattern. The shape of the eyes is important because that's where the cat's expression and character originate.
- Finish all of the continuous cuts with a #5 blade.
- Color the surface of the black segments with a black permanent marker; then, dip each colored segment in dark walnut stain. (**Note:** The dark parts of the ears are not black. Stain them using only one coat of dark walnut.)
- Work from the back of the image as you glue the segments in relief.
- The nose of the cat will be closest to you when he is viewed from the front. The mouth and eyes should be recessed slightly.
- Mount on an oval slab or display as is on a hardboard backer.

### Tools and Materials

- Light-colored, soft wood of choice (poplar), ½" to ¾" thick, sized to fit the pattern
- Scroll saw
- #5 reverse skip-tooth blades for general cuts
- #2 reverse skip-tooth blades for intricate cuts
- Temporary bond spray adhesive
- Drill or drill press
- 1/16" drill bit
- Sandpaper, small square of 120 grit
- Wax paper or butcher paper, large sheet
- Paper towels, one roll, or rags
- Small tongs or pliers
- Golden oak stain, one 32 oz. can
- Dark walnut stain, one 32 oz. can
- Colonial maple stain, one 32 oz. can
- Brushes, small and medium
- Black permanent marker
- Aluminum baking pans
- White acrylic paint or gesso
- Hot glue gun
- Glue sticks
- Wood glue, small bottle

Color black pieces with black marker. Then, dip them in dark walnut stain.

I used a dark walnut frame with a colonial maple backer to pick up the color of the cat's nose.

**Finished Size:** 10" x 13"
**Number of Pieces:** 120
**Enlarge 125%**

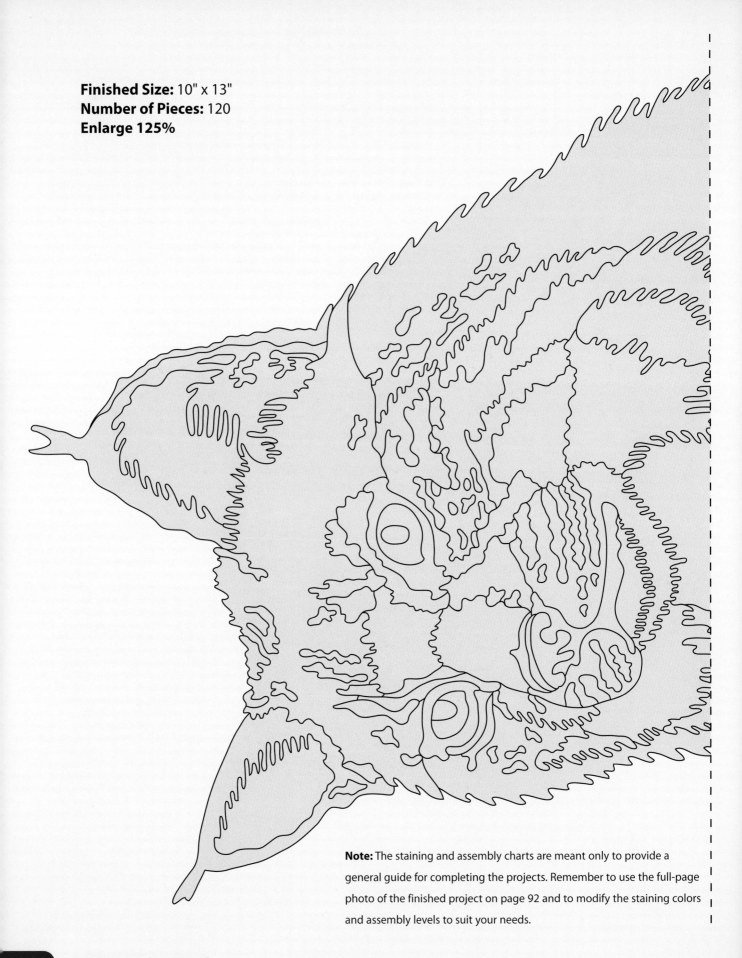

**Note:** The staining and assembly charts are meant only to provide a general guide for completing the projects. Remember to use the full-page photo of the finished project on page 92 and to modify the staining colors and assembly levels to suit your needs.

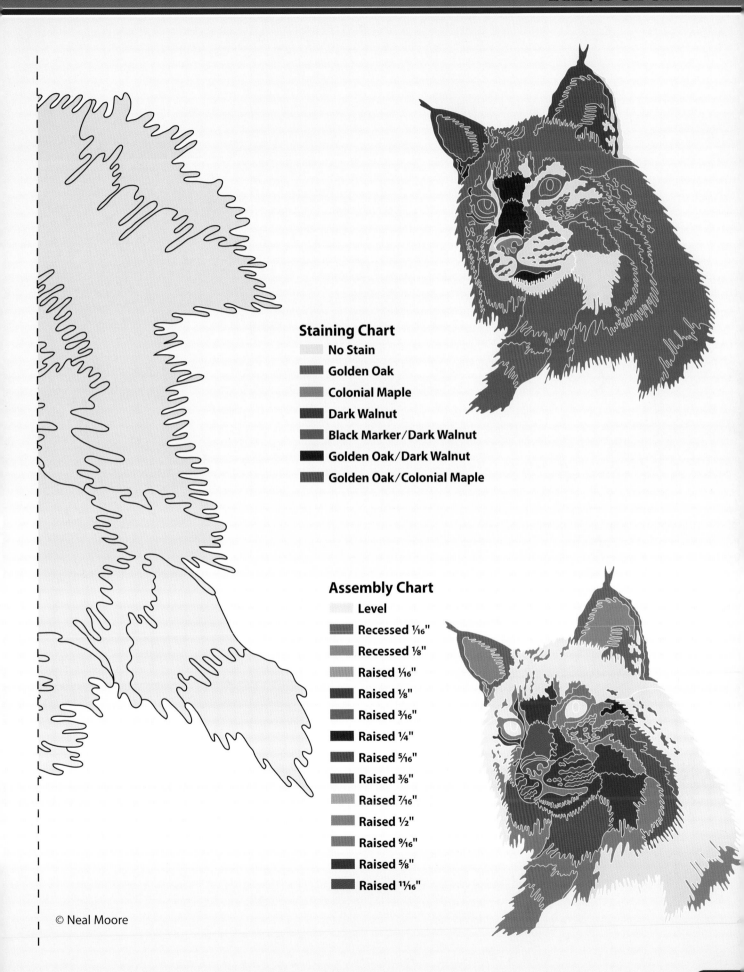

**Staining Chart**

- No Stain
- Golden Oak
- Colonial Maple
- Dark Walnut
- Black Marker/Dark Walnut
- Golden Oak/Dark Walnut
- Golden Oak/Colonial Maple

**Assembly Chart**

- Level
- Recessed ¹⁄₁₆"
- Recessed ⅛"
- Raised ¹⁄₁₆"
- Raised ⅛"
- Raised ³⁄₁₆"
- Raised ¼"
- Raised ⁵⁄₁₆"
- Raised ⅜"
- Raised ⁷⁄₁₆"
- Raised ½"
- Raised ⁹⁄₁₆"
- Raised ⅝"
- Raised ¹¹⁄₁₆"

© Neal Moore

# THE TIGER

Tigers are the largest members of the cat family and the only cats with striped fur. They are perfectly designed predators and possess beauty, grace, and awesome power. A tiger's presence in the wild is revealed by a paw print on a trail or a throaty roar, electrifying the forest and sending chills down the spine of all who share its domain. Humankind's admiration and fear of this great beast have made it a prominent figure in Asian myths, religions, arts, and imaginations.

Tigers were once found throughout the forested regions of tropical Asia, but hunting and habitat destruction have limited the tiger's range to isolated patches throughout Asia. To begin with this project, enlarge pattern to 140%.

- ◆ Light-colored, soft wood of choice (poplar), ½" to ¾" thick, sized to fit the pattern
- ◆ Scroll saw
- ◆ #5 reverse skip-tooth blades for general cuts
- ◆ #2 reverse skip-tooth blades for intricate cuts
- ◆ Temporary bond spray adhesive
- ◆ Drill or drill press
- ◆ ¹⁄₁₆" drill bit
- ◆ Sandpaper, small square of 120 grit
- ◆ Wax paper or butcher paper, large sheet
- ◆ Paper towels, one roll, or rags
- ◆ Small tongs or pliers
- ◆ Golden oak stain, one 32 oz. can
- ◆ Dark walnut stain, one 32 oz. can
- ◆ Colonial maple stain, one 32 oz. can
- ◆ Brushes, small and medium
- ◆ Black permanent marker
- ◆ Aluminum baking pans
- ◆ White acrylic paint or gesso
- ◆ Hot glue gun
- ◆ Glue sticks
- ◆ Wood glue, small bottle

## TIPS FOR COMPLETING THE PROJECT

- ◆ The tiger project consists of about 100 segments, and no mixing of stain is employed.
- ◆ Divide the pattern up into smaller segments.
- ◆ The nose is the only piece that is stained with colonial maple.
- ◆ Use aluminum pans and the slosh staining method to stain the pieces.
- ◆ The tiger's nose is the highest point, and the eyes have the lowest elevation.
- ◆ This project can be framed or displayed as is.

Notice the relief employed for the stripes on the tiger's forehead.

Start the final assembly and gluing from the top down.

**Note:** The staining and assembly charts are meant only to provide a general guide for completing the projects. Remember to use the full-page photo of the finished project on page 96 and to modify the staining colors and assembly levels to suit your needs.

**Finished Size:** 12½" x 9¾"
**Number of Pieces:** 104
**Enlarge 140%**

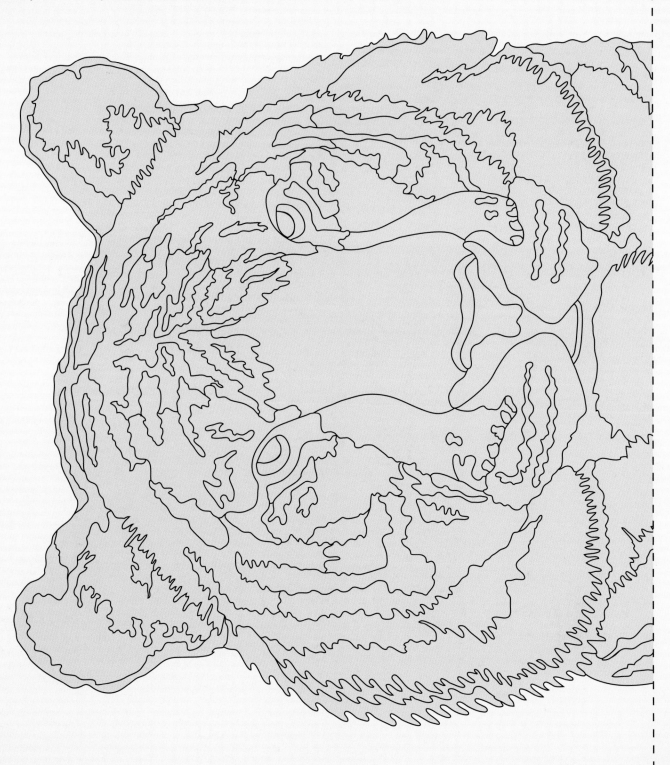

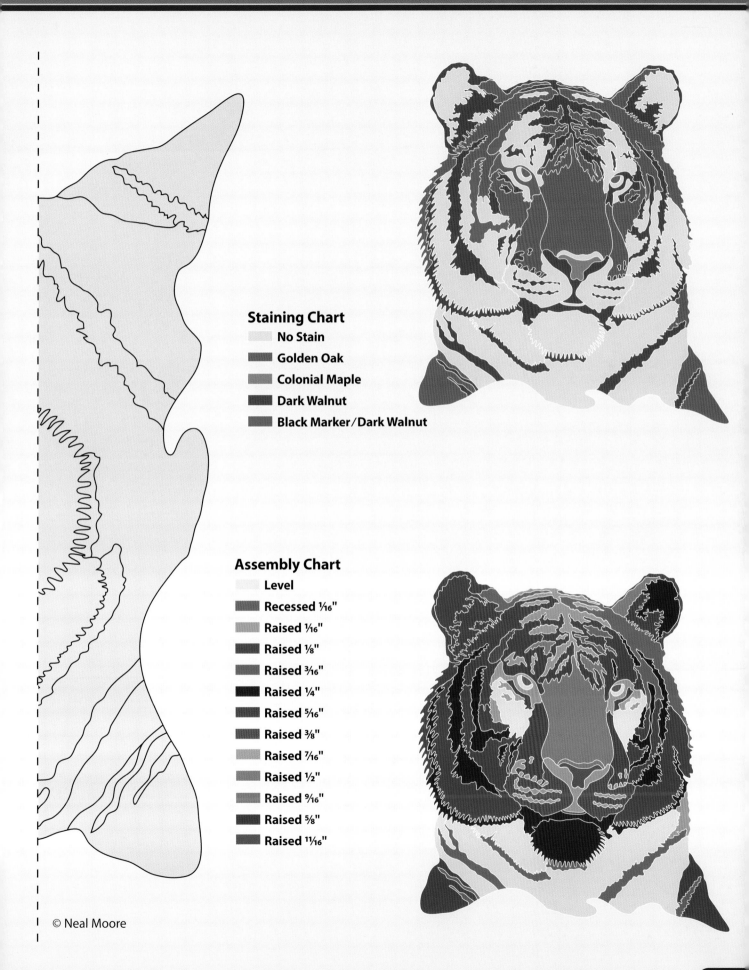

**Staining Chart**

No Stain
Golden Oak
Colonial Maple
Dark Walnut
Black Marker/Dark Walnut

**Assembly Chart**

Level
Recessed ¹⁄₁₆"
Raised ¹⁄₁₆"
Raised ¹⁄₈"
Raised ³⁄₁₆"
Raised ¹⁄₄"
Raised ⁵⁄₁₆"
Raised ³⁄₈"
Raised ⁷⁄₁₆"
Raised ¹⁄₂"
Raised ⁹⁄₁₆"
Raised ⁵⁄₈"
Raised ¹¹⁄₁₆"

© Neal Moore

# THE BEARS

Female grizzlies have their first young at about five to seven years of age. They can reproduce until almost 30 years of age, skipping three to four years between births. They generally avoid confrontations with humans, but sows with cubs will not hesitate to attack any perceived threat to their young.

Everyone who sees this portrait comments on the cub's smile. The cub in the photograph from which this pattern was developed appeared to be smiling, so I didn't alter his actual expression. To begin, enlarge the pattern to 130%.

## Tools and Materials

◆ Light-colored, soft wood of choice (poplar), ½" to ¾" thick, sized to fit the pattern
◆ Scroll saw
◆ #5 reverse skip-tooth blades for general cuts
◆ #2 reverse skip-tooth blades for intricate cuts
◆ Temporary bond spray adhesive
◆ Drill or drill press
◆ 1/16" drill bit
◆ Sandpaper, small square of 120 grit
◆ Wax paper or butcher paper, large sheet
◆ Paper towels, one roll, or rags
◆ Small tongs or pliers
◆ Golden oak stain, one 32 oz. can
◆ Dark walnut stain, one 32 oz. can
◆ Brushes, small and medium
◆ Black permanent marker
◆ Aluminum baking pans
◆ White acrylic paint or gesso
◆ Hot glue gun
◆ Glue sticks
◆ Wood glue, small bottle

## TIPS FOR COMPLETING THE PROJECT

◆ Cut the little cub first, removing the forehead and left ear to reach the center cuts.
◆ Dry fit the pieces as you go so segments won't be lost.
◆ Position all blade entry holes inside the pattern lines so they are less noticeable.
◆ Start cutting out the sow on the right side first.
◆ Treat the cub and the sow as two different projects when staining and gluing, but check the fit between the two when gluing. When each bear is glued tightly together, the spaces from the saw kerfs close, making the individual images slightly smaller and causing a wider kerf where the two bears join.
◆ The lighter-stained pieces are dipped in golden oak stain and then wiped off.
◆ Display this piece in a square frame constructed from false tread molding with a ¼" luan backing.

Cut the cub's forehead and left ear first.

Treat the cub as a separate project for staining and gluing.

**Finished Size:** 11" x 11⅝"
**Number of Pieces:** 69
**Enlarge 130%**

**Note:** The staining and assembly charts are meant only to provide a general guide for completing the projects. Remember to use the full-page photo of the finished project on page 100 and to modify the staining colors and assembly levels to suit your needs.

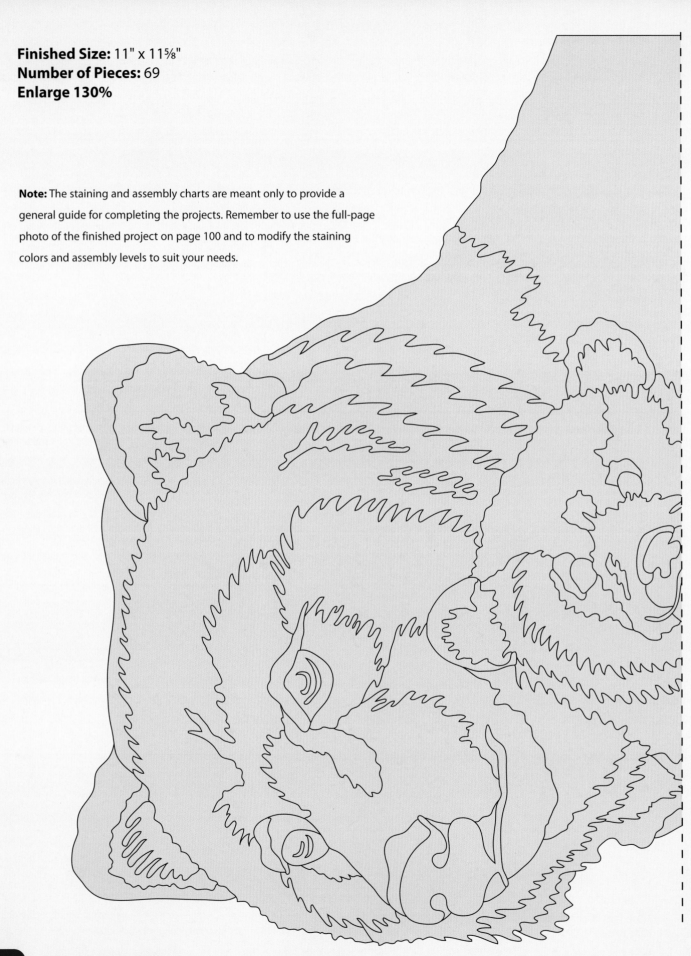

## Staining Chart

| | |
|---|---|
| | No Stain |
| | Golden Oak |
| | Dark Walnut |
| | Black Marker/Dark Walnut |
| | Golden Oak/Dark Walnut |

## Assembly Chart

| | |
|---|---|
| | Level |
| | Recessed 1/16" |
| | Recessed 1/8" |
| | Raised 1/16" |
| | Raised 1/8" |
| | Raised 3/16" |
| | Raised 1/4" |
| | Raised 5/16" |
| | Raised 3/8" |
| | Raised 7/16" |
| | Raised 1/2" |
| | Raised 9/16" |
| | Raised 5/8" |
| | Raised 11/16" |

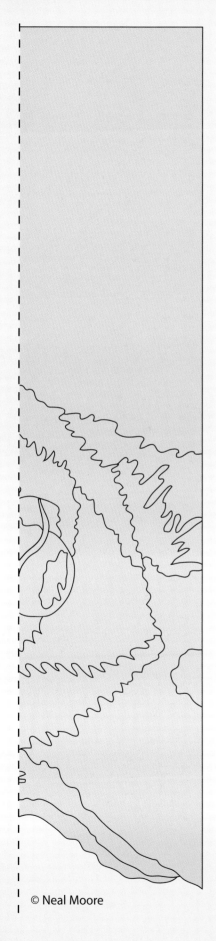

© Neal Moore

# THE ANTELOPE (IMPALA)

The impala is a slightly built antelope that populates the open woodlands of central and southern Africa. They travel in herds of at least 100 animals that scatter in a confusing burst of movement when challenged by a predator, such as a lion.

Male impalas, such as the one in this project, can be recognized by their long lyre-shaped horns. To begin, enlarge pattern to at least 140%. If you try to cut it smaller, you will encounter difficulties with the tiny white rings in the eyes.

## Tools and Materials

- Light-colored, soft wood of choice (poplar), ½" to ¾" thick, sized to fit the pattern
- Scroll saw
- #5 reverse skip-tooth blades for general cuts
- #2 reverse skip-tooth blades for intricate cuts
- Temporary bond spray adhesive
- Drill or drill press
- ¹⁄₁₆" drill bit
- Sandpaper, small square of 120 grit
- Wax paper or butcher paper, large sheet
- Paper towels, one roll, or rags
- Small tongs or pliers
- Golden oak stain, one 32 oz. can
- Dark walnut stain, one 32 oz. can
- Colonial maple stain, one 32 oz. can
- Brushes, small and medium
- Black permanent marker
- Aluminum baking pans
- White acrylic paint or gesso
- Hot glue gun
- Glue sticks
- Wood glue, small bottle

## TIPS FOR COMPLETING THE PROJECT

- Use a #2 blade to cut the eyes. All other segments can be cut with a #5 blade.
- Start by cutting the project into two pieces just under the eyes.
- Work from the outside in, in any order.
- Use wood glue to hold the spiraling horn segments together. They need additional strength because the finished project is displayed as is.
- Glue a ¼" x ¾" x 2" piece of plywood to the back of the forehead and attach a sawtooth picture hanger with small screws for display. The finished piece looks great with no frame or backing.

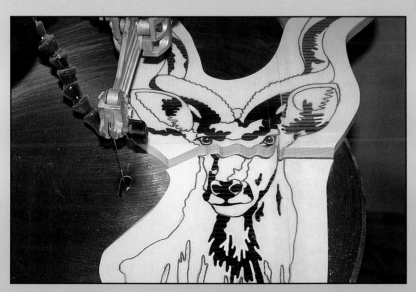

Cut the project into two pieces.

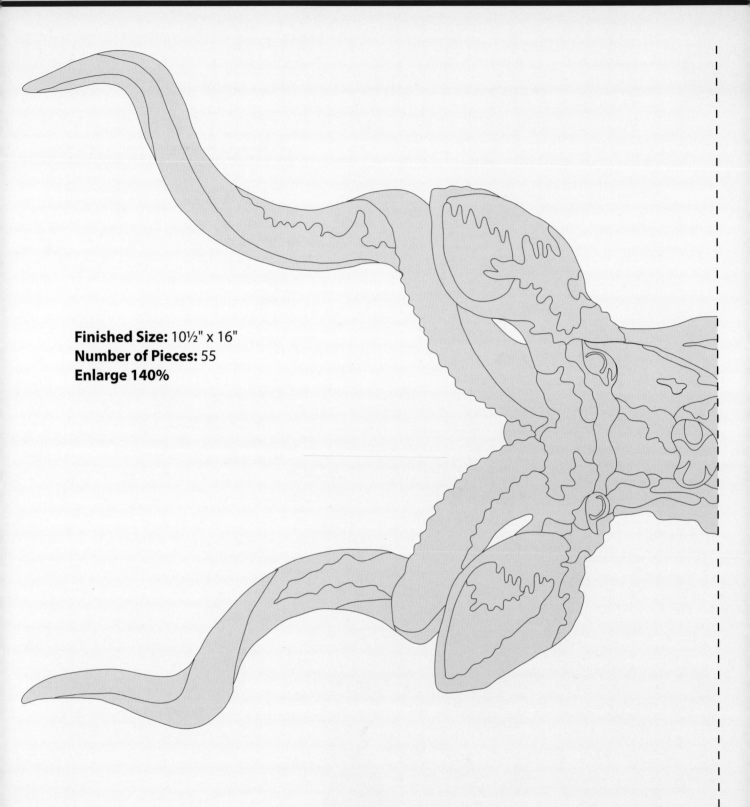

**Finished Size:** 10½" x 16"
**Number of Pieces:** 55
**Enlarge 140%**

**Note:** The staining and assembly charts are meant only to provide a general guide for completing the projects. Remember to use the full-page photo of the finished project on page 104 and to modify the staining colors and assembly levels to suit your needs.

## Staining Chart

No Stain
Golden Oak
Colonial Maple
Dark Walnut
Black Marker/Dark Walnut
Golden Oak/Dark Walnut

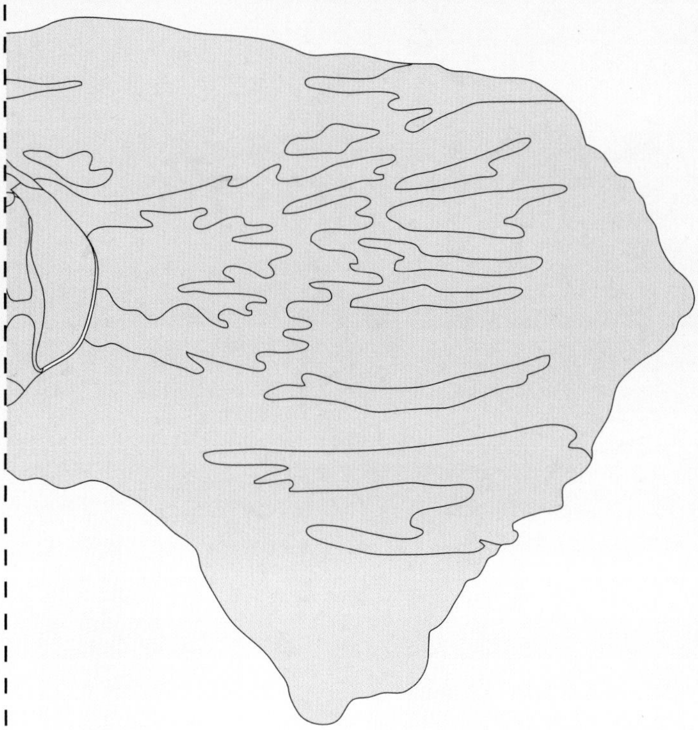

## Assembly Chart

Level
Raised ⅛"
Raised ³⁄₁₆"
Raised ¼"
Raised ⁵⁄₁₆"
Raised ⅜"
Raised ⁷⁄₁₆"
Raised ½"
Raised ⁹⁄₁₆"

© Neal Moore

# THE LION

A native of Africa, the male lion is one of the largest members of the cat family. Large males have been known to be eight feet in length and weigh 550 pounds. Their size and strength have captured human imagination since ancient times, giving rise to the nickname "king of beasts." Their mighty roar can be heard for up to five miles.

I chose this lion as a subject for a project because of the regal presence implied in the completed portrait. To begin, enlarge this pattern 190% to capture the full regal presence of this beautiful animal.

## Tools and Materials

- ◆ **Light-colored, soft wood of choice (poplar), ½" to ¾" thick, sized to fit the pattern**
- ◆ **Scroll saw**
- ◆ **#5 reverse skip-tooth blades for general cuts**
- ◆ **#2 reverse skip-tooth blades for intricate cuts**
- ◆ **Temporary bond spray adhesive**
- ◆ **Drill or drill press**
- ◆ **¹⁄₁₆" drill bit**
- ◆ **Sandpaper, small square of 120 grit**
- ◆ **Wax paper or butcher paper, large sheet**
- ◆ **Paper towels, one roll, or rags**
- ◆ **Small tongs or pliers**
- ◆ **Golden oak stain, one 32 oz. can**
- ◆ **Dark walnut stain, one 32 oz. can**
- ◆ **Brushes, small and medium**
- ◆ **Black permanent marker**
- ◆ **Aluminum baking pans**
- ◆ **White acrylic paint or gesso**
- ◆ **Hot glue gun**
- ◆ **Glue sticks**
- ◆ **Wood glue, small bottle**

## TIPS FOR COMPLETING THE PROJECT

- ◆ Plan your cuts carefully and cut the project into two or three smaller pieces.
- ◆ The pieces around the lion's eyes are the highest points, and the eyes have the lowest elevation.
- ◆ Display the lion on a luan backing mounted in a 22" x 23" frame.

The eyes should have the lowest elevation.

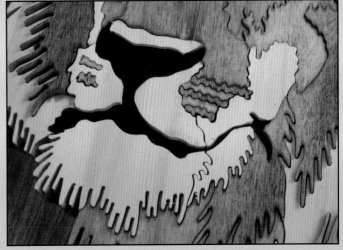

Notice how the lion's nose is not the highest point.

**Finished Size:** 15½" x 16½"
**Number of Pieces:** 69
**Enlarge 190%**

**Note:** The staining and assembly charts are meant only to provide a general guide for completing the projects. Remember to use the full-page photo of the finished project on page 108 and to modify the staining colors and assembly levels to suit your needs.

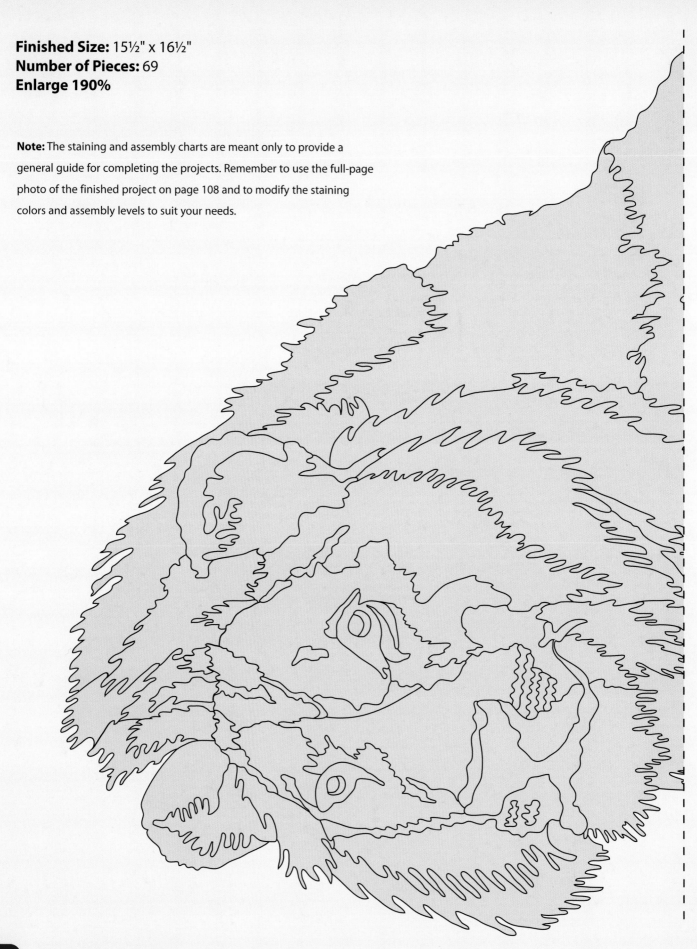

## Staining Chart

No Stain
Golden Oak
Dark Walnut
Black Marker/Dark Walnut
Golden Oak/Dark Walnut

## Assembly Chart

Level
Recessed ¹⁄₁₆"
Recessed ⅛"
Raised ¹⁄₁₆"
Raised ⅛"
Raised ³⁄₁₆"
Raised ¼"
Raised ⁵⁄₁₆"
Raised ⅜"
Raised ⁷⁄₁₆"
Raised ½"
Raised ⁹⁄₁₆"
Raised ⅝"
Raised ¹¹⁄₁₆"

© Neal Moore

# THE LIONESS

It's only fitting that the pattern for this stately lady be included to complement the lion portrait. Although the female lion is somewhat smaller than the male, most of the hunting chores for their social group, called a pride, fall on her.

Pride females care for cubs together, defend their hunting grounds, and protect the cubs from groups of adult males. The lioness is the real provider, and her attitude captured in this portrait shows it. To begin this project, enlarge the pattern to 130%.

## Tools and Materials

- ◆ Light-colored, soft wood of choice (poplar), ½" to ¾" thick, sized to fit the pattern
- ◆ Scroll saw
- ◆ #5 reverse skip-tooth blades for general cuts
- ◆ #2 reverse skip-tooth blades for intricate cuts
- ◆ Temporary bond spray adhesive
- ◆ Drill or drill press
- ◆ ¹⁄₁₆" drill bit
- ◆ Sandpaper, small square of 120 grit
- ◆ Wax paper or butcher paper, large sheet
- ◆ Paper towels, one roll, or rags
- ◆ Small tongs or pliers
- ◆ Golden oak stain, one 32 oz. can
- ◆ Dark walnut stain, one 32 oz. can
- ◆ Colonial maple stain, one 32 oz. can
- ◆ Brushes, small and medium
- ◆ Black permanent marker
- ◆ Aluminum baking pans
- ◆ White acrylic paint or gesso
- ◆ Hot glue gun
- ◆ Glue sticks
- ◆ Wood glue, small bottle

## TIPS FOR COMPLETING THE PROJECT

- ◆ Use colonial maple stain to highlight the area under the cat's right ear and in the eyes and to stain the nose.
- ◆ Frame the lioness in the same manner as the lion so they can be displayed as complementing pieces.
- ◆ The ridges around the lioness' eyes are the highest points, and the back neck piece has the lowest elevation.

Use colonial maple to highlight the eyes.

Colonial maple is also used for the nose.

**Finished Size:** 10" x 13½"
**Number of Pieces:** 82
**Enlarge 130%**

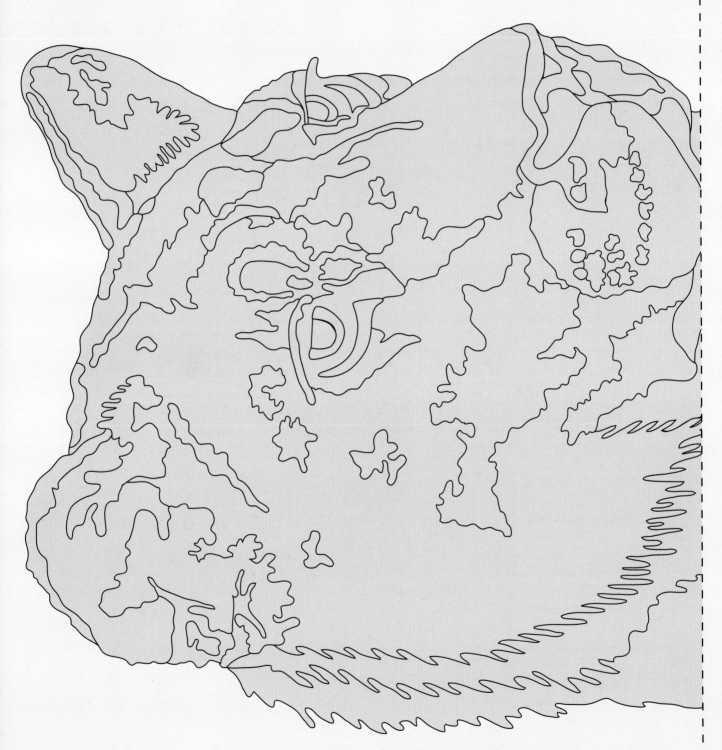

**Note:** The staining and assembly charts are meant only to provide a general guide for completing the projects. Remember to use the full-page photo of the finished project on page 112 and to modify the staining colors and assembly levels to suit your needs.

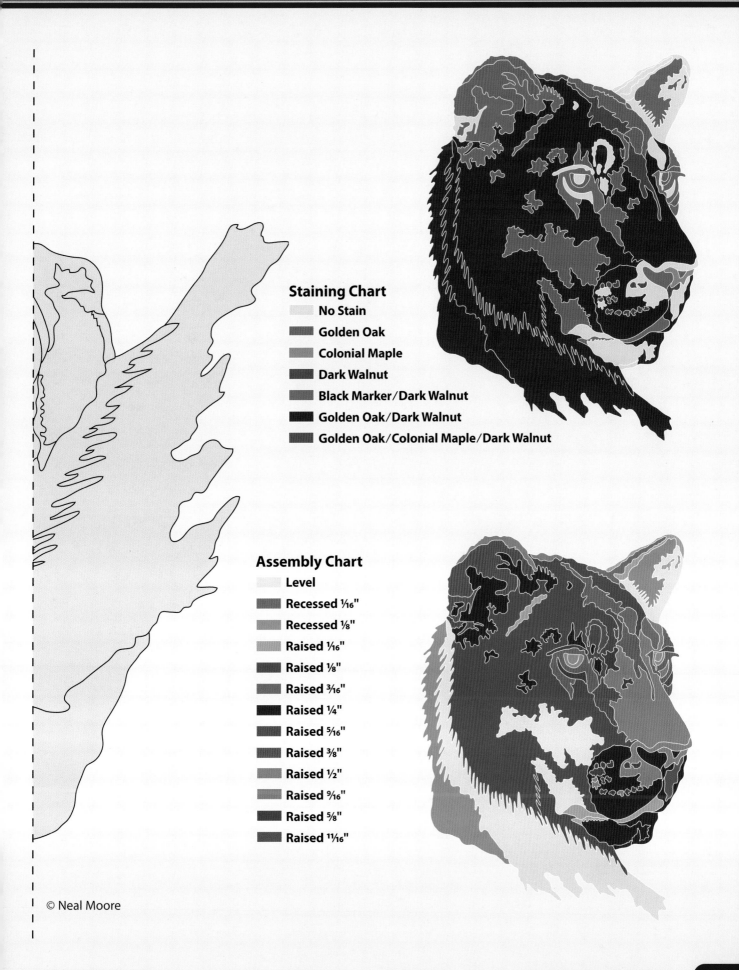

**Staining Chart**

No Stain
Golden Oak
Colonial Maple
Dark Walnut
Black Marker/Dark Walnut
Golden Oak/Dark Walnut
Golden Oak/Colonial Maple/Dark Walnut

**Assembly Chart**

Level
Recessed 1/16"
Recessed 1/8"
Raised 1/16"
Raised 1/8"
Raised 3/16"
Raised 1/4"
Raised 5/16"
Raised 3/8"
Raised 1/2"
Raised 9/16"
Raised 5/8"
Raised 11/16"

© Neal Moore

# THE CHEETAH

The cheetah is one of the fastest land animals in the world. It can accelerate to 58 miles per hour in two to three seconds. These African animals have decreased dramatically in numbers due to the illegal market for their beautiful coats.

I really liked this particular cat's eyes in the original photograph, so I tried to capture the expression in the portrait. To begin, enlarge the pattern at least 180% to get the cheetah near life size. The pattern for this project differs slightly from the finished piece. When I completed the project, I wasn't happy with the cheetah's nose. I changed the pattern for this book so your portrait will look more realistic.

## Tools and Materials

- ◆ Light-colored, soft wood of choice (poplar), ½" to ¾" thick, sized to fit the pattern
- ◆ Scroll saw
- ◆ #5 reverse skip-tooth blades for general cuts
- ◆ #2 reverse skip-tooth blades for intricate cuts
- ◆ Temporary bond spray adhesive
- ◆ Drill or drill press
- ◆ ¹⁄₁₆" drill bit
- ◆ Sandpaper, small square of 120 grit
- ◆ Wax paper or butcher paper, large sheet
- ◆ Paper towels, one roll, or rags
- ◆ Small tongs or pliers
- ◆ 2 pieces ¼" x 24" x 24" luan plywood, or stiff cardboard
- ◆ Golden oak stain, one 32 oz. can
- ◆ Dark walnut stain, one 32 oz. can
- ◆ Brushes, small and medium
- ◆ Black permanent marker
- ◆ Aluminum baking pans
- ◆ White acrylic paint or gesso
- ◆ Hot glue gun
- ◆ Glue sticks

## TIPS FOR COMPLETING THE PROJECT

- ◆ Drill blade entry holes inside the spots and touching the pattern lines so the stain will conceal the holes.
- ◆ Stain all of the spots with golden oak, heavily smear mixed with dark walnut.
- ◆ Stain the face golden oak. When dry, dry brush highlights on the bridge of the nose, the cheeks, and the forehead with colonial maple stain.
- ◆ The nose has the highest elevation.
- ◆ All spots are elevated about ¹⁄₁₆".
- ◆ Display the cheetah in a dark frame with a light backer.

Elevate all spots ¹⁄₁₆".

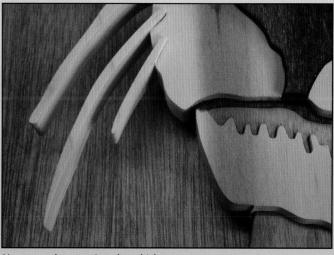

Use care when cutting the whiskers.

**Finished Size:** 15½" x 17½"
**Number of Pieces:** 140
**Enlarge 180%**

**Note:** The staining and assembly charts are meant only to provide a general guide for completing the projects. Remember to use the full-page photo of the finished project on page 116 and to modify the staining colors and assembly levels to suit your needs.

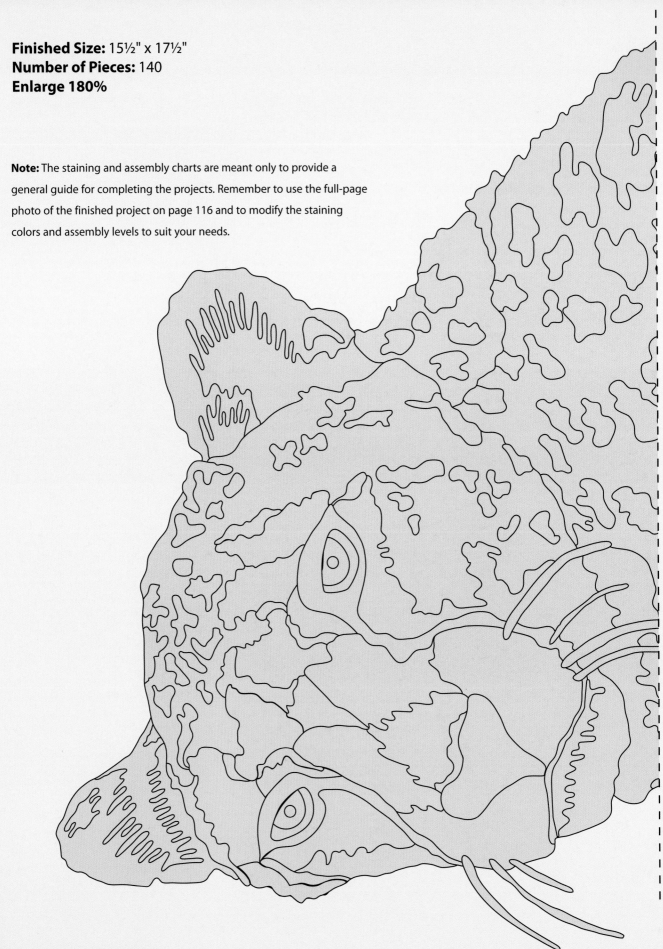

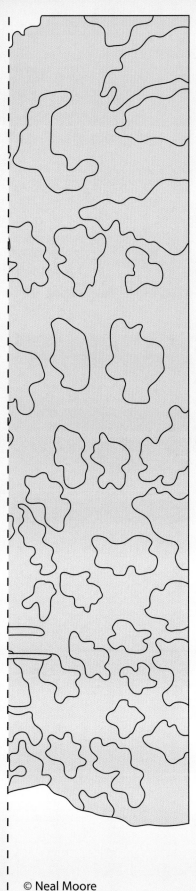

## Staining Chart

No Stain

Golden Oak

Dark Walnut

Black Marker/Dark Walnut

Golden Oak/Dark Walnut

## Assembly Chart

Level

Recessed ¹⁄₁₆"

Recessed ⅛"

Raised ¹⁄₁₆"

Raised ⅛"

Raised ³⁄₁₆"

Raised ¼"

Raised ⁵⁄₁₆"

Raised ⅜"

Raised ⁷⁄₁₆"

Raised ½"

Raised ⁹⁄₁₆"

Raised ⅝"

Raised ¹¹⁄₁₆"

© Neal Moore

# More Great Project Books from Fox Chapel Publishing

**Animal Puzzles for the Scroll Saw**

*By Judy and Dave Peterson*

**$14.95**
1-56523-255-0

**Fantasy & Legend Scroll Saw Puzzles**

*By Judy and Dave Peterson*

**$14.95**
1-56523-256-9

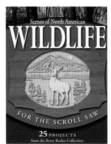

**Scenes of North American Wildlife for the Scroll Saw**

*By Rick and Karen Longabaugh*

**$16.95**
1-56523-277-1

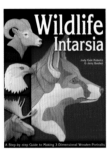

**Wildlife Intarsia**

*By Judy Gale Roberts and Jerry Booher*

**$19.95**
1-56523-282-8

**Great Book of Woodburning**

*By Lora S. Irish*

**$19.95**
1-56523-287-9

**Box-Making Projects for the Scroll Saw**

*By Gary MacKay*

**$17.95**
1-56523-294-1

## LOOK FOR THESE BOOKS AT YOUR LOCAL BOOK STORE OR WOODWORKING RETAILER

### Or call 800-457-9112 • Visit www.FoxChapelPublishing.com

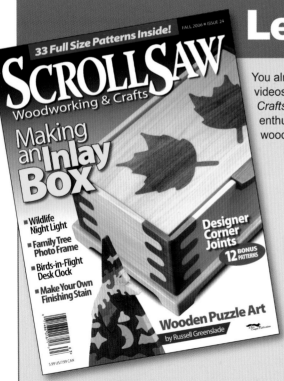

# Learn from the Experts

You already know that Fox Chapel Publishing is a leading source for woodworking books, videos, and DVDs, but did you know that we also publish *Scroll Saw Woodworking & Crafts*? Published quarterly, *Scroll Saw Woodworking & Crafts* is the magazine scroll saw enthusiasts turn to for the premium projects and expert information from today's leading wood crafters. **Contact us today for your free trial issue!**

# SCROLLSAW
## Woodworking & Crafts

■ Written by today's leading scroll saw artists

■ Dozens of attractive, shop-tested patterns and project ideas for scrollers of all skill levels

■ Great full-color photos of step-by-step projects and completed work, presented in a clear, easy-to-follow format

■ Keep up with what's new in the scrolling community with tool reviews, artist profiles, and event coverage

**Subscribe Today!**   888-840-8590 • www.scrollsawer.com